INSIGHT GUIDES

VENICE
smart guide

Discovery CHANNEL

APA PUBLICATIONS L
Part of the Langenscheidt Publishing Group

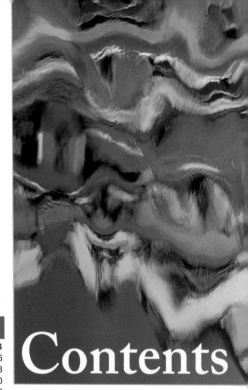

Contents

Areas

A–Z

Below: gondoliers waiting for custom.

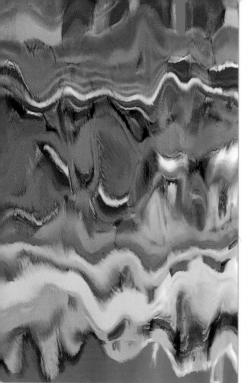

Left: dreamy reflections in ancient canals.

Atlas

Below: Paolo Veronese's Trionfo di Venezia.

Venice

A city that has inspired artists and travellers for centuries, Venice is a canvas for a multitude of fantasies. You can walk in Casanova's footsteps, sleep in Hemingway's bed, or explore the world of Marco Polo in his home city. You will soon discover why one of the world's greatest maritime powers has become one of the world's greatest tourist attractions.

Venice Facts and Figures

Population: **61,000**

Visitors per year: **15 million**

Length of lagoon: **51km**

Height above sea level: **1m**

Number of canals: **160**

Number of bridges: **430**

Number of churches: **107**

Visitors who only visit San Marco: **50 percent**

Height of the Campanile: **100m**

Height of worst flood (1966): **0.9m above ground level**

Average age of Venetian: **45**

Number of Grand Canal palaces: **over 200**

By Foot and Ferry

The only city in the world built entirely on water, Venice is divided into six districts *(sestieri)*, all with very different characters. This guide will introduce you to them all, and outline a *vaporetto* (ferry) trip along the Grand Canal. As well as encompassing many of the city's architectural glories, this will give you an idea of the layout of the city. Despite its watery character, you will find that you can get around most of the city on foot, with occasional trips on ferries for circling the city or taking you to the far corners of the lagoon.

On foot, if you leave behind the crowds of San Marco, you will soon find yourself immersed in a warren of narrow alleys, back canals and rambling *campi* (squares). Wherever you go there will be cafés where you can linger alfresco, or tiny *bacari* (bars) where you can enjoy a glass of wine and Venetian tapas.

City Neighbourhoods

Piazza San Marco is everybody's starting point. The beautifully proportioned square that Napoleon termed 'the finest drawing room in Europe' is the site of the great Basilica, the Doge's Palace and gracious cafés. To the north and east of San Marco lies Castello, which offers a slice of everyday life, as dark alleys open onto bright, bustling squares. The area is home to several major churches, as well as Arsenale, the great military and naval complex founded in the 12th century.

San Polo and Santa Croce are two adjoining districts that encompass the labyrinthine Rialto market, the famous Rialto bridge that traditionally divided the city and the Frari, the greatest of all Venetian Gothic churches.

Cannaregio is the most densely populated district, but it's home to some lovely churches as well as the former Jewish Ghetto. Dorsoduro is the *sestiere* for some delightful walks along the Zattere quayside, as well as visits to La Salute church, the Accademia and the Peggy Guggenheim collection of modern art.

Islands of the Lagoon

For those who have time, there are the islands to explore, easily reached by frequent ferries. Murano is famous for its glass-making, Burano

Below: gondolas along Riva degli Schiavoni.

for its lace and its colourful fishermen's cottages, and Torcello for its cathedral, the oldest monument in the lagoon. Giudecca, an island that is undergoing a rebirth, is home to Il Redentore church, a Palladian masterpiece, and the most luxurious hotel in Venice, the Cipriani. San Giorgio Maggiore is the site of a famous Benedictine monastery; while the Lido, a long strip of land between the city and the Adriatic, glories in its role as a superior film set.

Venice in Peril

Venice officially stopped sinking in 1983. The biggest watery threats now are *acqua alta* (high water) and wave damage from boats to the foundations of buildings. During autumn and winter duck boards are a familiar sight in low-lying Piazza San Marco. Work is now going ahead on the hugely controversial Moses project, the mobile flood barriers which will close off the lagoon during the high tides. Environmentalists are trying to halt the project; even those in favour see it merely as a means of buying time. Meanwhile rocketing house prices (driven up by foreign buyers) are forcing Venetians out to cheaper accommodation on the mainland. Since 1966 the population has halved from 121,000 to 61,000. If the exodus continues at the present rate there will be no Venetians left by the mid 21st century and Venice (assuming it still stands) will become Italy's Disneyland.

Highlights

▲ **The Rialto Bridge** This graceful bridge spanning the Grand Canal, is at the heart of the bustling Rialto district, famous for its labyrinthine market.

▼ **The Doge's Palace** A masterpiece of elegant High Gothic style.

▲ **The Accademia** Giorgione's *Tempest*, one of many sumptuous masterpieces in this great showcase of Venetian art.

▲ **Murano** and **Burano** Colourful lagoon islands. ▶ **Basilica di San Marco** The grandest private chapel in the world.

▶ **Scuola Grande di San Rocco** Grand 16th-century *scuola*, home to Titian's poetic *Annunciation*. Opposite, **I Frari**, the greatest of all Venetian Gothic churches, holds the painter's tomb.

Piazza San Marco

Piazza San Marco, which Napoleon would later call 'the finest drawing room in Europe', acted as the heart of the Venetian republic. Elegantly proportioned, with colonnades on three sides, fringed with exquisite monuments (most dating from the 16th and 17th centuries) it is an architectural delight. Full of people and pigeons, free of traffic and lined with grand cafés, St Mark's Square is a wonderful place to sit and watch the world go by. After braving the hordes in the Basilica – the glorious centrepiece of the square – retreat to the Caffè Florian or the Caffè Quadri for a prosecco or a Bellini in style.

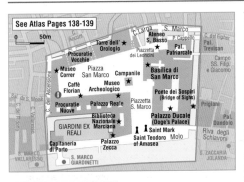

See Atlas Pages 138-139

0   50m

C. Larga   S. Marco
Ancora   Ateneo   C. del Figher
Torre dell'   S. Basso   P. Cappello   Pal.
Orologio   Piazzetta   Pal.   Trevisan
Procuratie   dei Leoncini   Patriarcale
Vecchie   Campo
Museo   Piazza   Campanile   Basilica di   SS. Filip.
Correr   San Marco   San Marco   e Giacomo
Caffè   Museo
Florian   Archeologico
Procuratie   Ponte dei Sospiri
Nuove   Palazzo Reale   (Bridge of Sighs)
Biblioteca   Piazzetta   Prigioni
Nazionale   S. Marco
GIARDINI EX   Marciana   Palazzo Ducale   Pal.
REALI   Saint Mark   (Doge's Palace)   Dandolo
Saint Teodoro   Riva degli
Capitaneria   Palazzo   of Amasea   Molo   Schiavoni
di Porto   Zecca
S. MARCO   S. MARCO   S. ZACCARIA
VALLARESSO   GIARDINETTI   JOLANDA

The piazza floods frequently every winter and duckboards are laid down so that people can cross without getting wet feet. It is a novelty for tourists, but something of a headache for the city authorities.

a trumpeting angel swing out from the face of the Clock Tower on the stroke of every hour and rotate around a gilded Madonna. The tower has recently reopened after many years of restoration.

Basilica di San Marco

The jewel in the crown is the **Basilica di San Marco**, shrine of the Republic and symbol of Venetian glory. This exquisite building encapsulates the old Republic's vision of itself as the successor to Constantinople. Despite an eclectic mix of styles and domes of unequal proportions, San Marco conveys a sense of grandeur as well as a jewel-like delicacy. SEE ALSO CHURCHES, P.38.

Torre dell'Orologio

The graceful Clock Tower features a splendid zodiacal clock that shows the time in both Arabic and Roman numerals. At Epiphany (6 January) and Ascension week in May, three Magi and

Campanile

For the most breathtaking views of the Piazza and the city, take a lift to the top of the 100m Bell Tower, which is the tallest building in Venice. SEE ALSO MONUMENTS, P.70

Palazzo Ducale

The **Doge's Palace** was the power house of Venice, the residence of the doges and seat of government. The shimmering pink façade, the delicate arches and florid Gothic detail conceal an equally flamboyant interior. The baroque **Ponte dei Sospiri** – the legendary Bridge of Sighs – linked the palace with the notorious city prison across the canal. SEE ALSO PALAZZI, P.93–5

Left: the top of the Campanile.

Left: the domes and shimmering façade of San Marco.

Caffè Florian

This is the best-known and most elegant of the Piazza's grand cafés. It's famous for lush, opulent décor, for tables outside under colonnades, schmaltzy music and expensive drinks. The neighbouring **Caffè Quadri** comes a close second in all these respects.
SEE ALSO BARS AND CAFÉS P.30

Columns of San Marco and San Teodoro

The Piazzetta (Little Square), overlooking the waterfront, is framed by two soaring granite columns. One is crowned by a statue of St Theodore, the original patron saint of Venice, the other by a winged lion of St Mark. Public executions used to take place between the pillars.
SEE ALSO MONUMENTS P.70

Piazzetta dei Leoncini

The tiny square beside the Basilica di San Marco is named after the long-suffering pair of marble lions who guard it, and who have been used as play horses by countless generations of children.

> When the Campanile collapsed in 1902, the city council decided to rebuild it as it was, where it was. In 1912, 1,000 years after the first watchtower was built, it was completed.

Museo Correr

Opposite the Basilica, at the far end of the Piazza, the **Museo Correr** is home to the city museum and contains artefacts from every aspect of Venice's history. It also houses a fine collection of 14th- to 16th-century paintings, including a room of works by Jacopo Bellini and his sons. The core collection of the **Museo Archeologico** (accessed through the Museo Correr) consists of Greek and Roman sculpture that influenced generations of Venetian artists who came to study here. Set in an extended loggia is the **Biblioteca Nazionale Marciana** (also accessed through the Museo Correr). The library, built in 1537, is also known as the Libreria Sansoviniana after its architect, Jacopo Sansovino. Derived from Roman classical architecture, it was considered one of the greatest works of its day. Beside the library the severe-looking **Zecca** (the Mint) was also designed by Sansovino.
SEE ALSO MONUMENTS, P.70; MUSEUMS & GALLERIES P.75

Below: *acqua alta* and duck boards on Piazza San Marco.

Sestiere San Marco

Although overshadowed by the attractions of Piazza San Marco, this *sestiere* (district) is noted for its bustling *campi* (squares) and the maze-like Mercerie, a fascinating shopping quarter to the north of St Mark's Square. It is also home to some of the finest palaces along the Grand Canal. This loop of the major waterway occupied by San Marco is known as the 'seven *campi* between the bridges'; a succession of theatrical spaces, each with inviting bars. The most celebrated of these is the clubby, crowded and cosmopolitan Harry's Bar, birthplace of the Bellini cocktail.

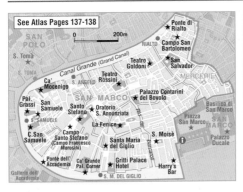

Above: a Venetian institution.

Harry's Bar

This legendary, but resolutely un-glitzy watering hole on Calle Vallaresso is known as the best bar in the best city in the world. Over the years, classic cocktails and a great atmosphere have drawn prominent personalities, from Churchill and Chaplin to Fellini and Sinatra. The *calle* on which it stands is lined with designer boutiques and is the hub of a chic shopping district, embracing the **Ridotto**, once Venice's licentious

Giuseppe Cipriani, who founded Harry's Bar in 1931, created the famous Bellini cocktail: a mixture of fresh peach juice and sparkling prosecco. The Bar is still run by the Cipriani family.

casino for masked revellers, but now restored and part of the **Monaco e Grand Hotel**. SEE ALSO BARS AND CAFÉS, P.30; HOTELS, P.61

Gritti Palace Hotel

John Ruskin, the art critic and aesthete (1819–1900), wrote his influential *Stones of Venice* while staying in this famous Venetian palace hotel *(see also the Hotel Daniele, p.62)*. The Gritti terrace offers a grandstand view of the Grand Canal and the church of **La Salute**, which lies diagonally opposite. On the adjoining square north of the hotel, the Baroque church (1678-83) of **Santa Maria Zobenigo** was built to the glory of the male members of the Barbaro family and their

militaristic pursuits. SEE ALSO CHURCHES, P.39; HOTELS, P.60

La Fenice

The famous opera house was first destroyed by fire in 1838 but rose again from the ashes like the phoenix *(fenice)*. In 1996 it was again the victim of a major fire, but has since been restored to its former glory and reopened in 2004, with a celebratory performance of *La Traviata*. Atmospheric bars can be found tucked around encircling canals. SEE ALSO MUSIC, P.84

Campo Santo Stefano

After Piazza San Marco this is the noblest of the squares and one of the most diverting

Left: gamblers in *Il Ridotto*. Venice still enjoys a reputation as a city for pleasure seekers.

If you enjoy opera, and are here during the opera season from autumn to early summer, it's worth trying to get tickets for La Fenice (tel: 041-2424 or book online at www.teatrolafenice.it).

of Carlo Goldoni, the city's most famous playwright.

Mercerie

The shadowy maze of alleys running between the Rialto and Piazza San Marco was named after the haberdashers' shops that once lined the route. Today it remains an engaging bazaar where you can buy such traditional souvenirs as marbled paper, Murano glass, leather goods and carnival masks.

places to watch people going about their daily lives. Lined with palaces and cafés, it is the setting for a chic *passeggiata* every evening. At the northern end of the square stands the Gothic church of **Santo Stefano**. The square makes a seamless link with the Dorsoduro's **Galleria dell' Accademia** *(see p.21)*, the great gallery of Venetian art on the far side of the bridge.
SEE ALSO CHURCHES, P.39

Campo San Samuele

This engaging quarter on the bend of the canal was Casanova's parish, with Lord Byron's former home nearby, in **Ca' Mocenigo**, overlooking the Grand Canal. San Samuele, Casanova's baptismal church, is graced with a Byzantine bell tower. Beside the ferry landing-stage looms the formidable **Palazzo Grassi**, which has recently re-opened as a major exhibition centre.
SEE ALSO PALAZZI, P.96

Palazzo Contarini del Bovolo

Concealed in a maze of alleys between Calle Vida and Calle Contarini, this late-Gothic palace is celebrated for its romantic arcaded staircase, which is linked to loggias of brick and smooth white stone.
SEE ALSO PALAZZI, P.92–3

Campo San Bartolomeo

A popular evening rendezvous with cafés, bars and a statue

San Salvador

On the far side of Rio di San Salvador the church is a fine example of Venetian Renaissance architecture, containing two masterpieces by Titian. The cloisters are now the setting of the **Telecom Italia Future Centre**, a high-tech museum. This is a perfect place for children to while away an hour or two, and admission is free.
SEE ALSO CHILDREN, P.36

Below: Sunday morning on the Campo Santo Stefano.

Canale Grande

Nearly 4km long and up to 70m wide, the surprisingly shallow Grand Canal is spanned by five bridges and lined with over 200 sumptuous palaces. This great waterway sweeps through the six city districts (*sestieri*), its switchback shape providing changing vistas of palaces and churches, warehouses and markets. Once a waterway for merchant vessels and great galleys, the canal now welcomes simpler craft from gondolas to garbage barges. Purchase a day pass and trail up and down the Canal to your heart's content, stopping at sights as the fancy takes you (*vaporetto* lines 1 – better because it's slower – and 82 both cover the route).

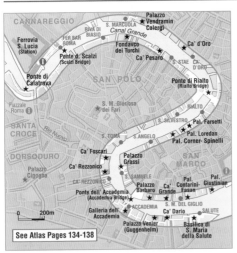

From San Marco to the Accademia Bridge

From the Vallaresso stop, the *vaporetto* sweeps into St Mark's Basin with romantic views across to **San Giorgio Maggiore**. Set on the right bank, the Gothic showpiece **Palazzo Giustinian** is the first significant palace. It is the headquarters of the Biennale exhibition organisation. On the left bank, the Baroque basilica of **La Salute** marks the entrance to the Grand Canal. On the opposite bank, the **Palazzo Contarini-Fasan** is a tiny, exquisite, 15th-century palace traditionally known as Desdemona's house. Several palaces further down on the left bank, the gently listing **Ca' Dario** is one of the loveliest palaces on the Canal. Henry James adored its 'little marble plates and sculptured circles'. On the right bank looms **Ca' Grande**, a monumental classical palace built by Sansovino, now the seat of the provincial government. Facing Ca' Grande is the **Palazzo Venier** an incongruous squat white structure, home to the **Peggy Guggenheim Collection of Modern Art**. Just before the Accademia Bridge stands the **Palazzo Barbaro**,

Left: the Rialto Market.

Left: La Salute.

At the next bend is the iconic single-span **Rialto Bridge**. It is a good place to stop for a bite to eat at one of the neighbourhood *bacari*. Beyond the Rialto, on the right bank, the **Ca' d'Oro** is generally regarded as the loveliest Gothic palace on the Grand Canal, with its oriental pinnacles and ethereal tracery and home to **Galleria Franchetti**.
SEE ALSO MUSEUMS AND GALLERIES, P.78

Ca' Pesaro to the Station

The **Ca' Pesaro** is a stately Baroque palace. It has an inner courtyard lined with balconies and loggias, and is home to the **Museo d'Arte Orientale** and the **Galleria d'Arte Moderna**. Further along on the right bank the **Palazzo Vendramin Calergi** is another Renaissance gem. Wagner died here in 1883. It is now home to the city's casino. The last stop on this Grand Canal tour is the **Fondaco dei Turchi**, an arcaded Veneto-Byzantine building and former trading base for Turkish merchants. Today it is home to the **Museo di Storia Naturale**. Carry on and you'll reach the station.
SEE ALSO MONUMENTS, P.71; MUSEUMS AND GALLERIES, P.76–7

The greatest canal festival is Festa della Madonna della Salute (21 Nov), when a pontoon bridge to La Salute church is created, to celebrate the city's deliverance from plague in 1630.

---

a fine Gothic palace renowned for the eminent guests who stayed here, among them Monet, Whistler and Henry James. The distinctive wooden **Accademia Bridge** is a popular meeting place.
SEE ALSO MUSEUMS AND GALLERIES, P.78–9

The Accademia to Ca' Foscari

Ca' Rezzonico on the left bank is a Baroque masterpiece, which is home to the fascinating **Museo del Settecento Veneziano** (Museum of 18th-Century Life). On the right bank, the imposing 18th-century residence of **Palazzo Grassi** has been converted into a slick international exhibition showcase. A little further along is the 15th-century **Ca' Foscari** described by the art historian, John Ruskin, as the 'noblest example in Venice of 15th-century Gothic'.
SEE ALSO MUSEUMS AND GALLERIES, P.77

Ca' Foscari to Ca' d'Oro

Around the bend, on the right bank, beside the Sant'Angelo stop, is **Palazzo Corner-Spinelli**. This magnificent Renaissance palace, with its double-arched windows, became a prototype for other *palazzi* in Venice. As the boat stops at San Silvestro look across the canal to appreciate the **Palazzo Farsetti** and **Palazzo Loredan**, two of the city's finest Veneto-Byzantine palaces.

For more information on individual Palazzi listed here, see p.92–101; churches are covered in greater detail on p.38–45

Below: Grand Canal gondolier.

Castello

Lying to the east of San Marco, Castello is a mix of sophistication and low-key charm, and offers a slice of local life. It is home to the city's best-known waterfront, to Vivaldi's church, and the most mysterious confraternity seat in Venice. In its eastern reaches, a working-class district, lie the Arsenale, the shipyard where the great Venetian galleys were built and the Giardini Pubblici, where the Biennale is staged. As the most varied Venetian *sestiere*, it offers a spectrum of sights from the sophisticated bustle along Riva degli Schiavoni to the quaint fishing-village ambience of San Pietro.

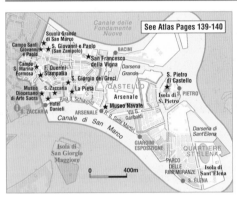

See Atlas Pages 139-140

Above: Italian naval officers outside the Arsenale.

Riva degli Schiavoni

Now bustling with tourists and souvenir sellers, this sweeping quayside once thronged with Dalmatian sailors from Schiavonia, modern day Croatia, who moored their boats along the waterfront. It was widened and paved in 1782 and has been a popular Venetian promenade ever since. As a hub of upmarket tourism, it is lined with distinguished hotels, all vying for cocktail clientele. The **Hotel Danieli** is the most historic hotel in Venice, having occupied the Gothic Palazzo Dandolo since 1822. Illustrious visitors have included Wagner, Ruskin, Balzac, Proust and Dickens. The rooftop terrace remains a superb place for a drink at any time of the day.

Behind the Riva and the Doge's Palace, **Museo Diocesano di Arte Sacra** is home to works of art from deconsecrated churches and adjoins the peaceful Romanesque cloister of Sant' Apollonia, with sculptural fragments from St Mark's Basilica.

Back on the waterfront, east of the Hotel Danieli, the church of **La Pietà** was once the backdrop for concerts by a choir of orphan girls under Vivaldi's tutelage. After his

> The Chapel of the Rosary in the north transept of Santi Giovanni e Paolo was built to commemorate the Venetian victory over the Turks in 1571 at the Battle of Lepanto.

death in 1741, it became the city's leading concert hall.
SEE ALSO CHURCHES, P.41–2; HOTELS P.62; MUSEUMS AND GALLERIES, P.80; RESTAURANTS, P.110

Sacred Art and Architecture

Away from the quayside are serveral churches of note. The delightful church of **San Zaccaria** is graced by Coducci's curvilinear facade; a Renaissance masterpiece that conceals an older basilica. The church is home to a superb altarpiece of the *Madonna and Child* by Giovanni Bellini.

The Greek Orthodox church of **San Giorgio dei Greci** is distinctive for the alarming tilt of its bell tower. The Greeks are one of the

Left: not all canals are used exclusively for tourism.

nificent Gothic church and Renaissance *scuola* and the setting of Verrochio's magnificent equestrian statue of Bartolomeo Colleoni.

More familiarly known as San Zanipolo, **Santi Giovanni e Paolo** is a huge, austere church founded in the late 13th century. The Gothic pinnacles can be seen from both banks of the Grand Canal, with the roof line displaying statues of Dominican saints. Known as the Pantheon of Venice, it contains the tombs of 25 doges.

A former meeting house of silk dealers and goldsmiths, the **Scuola Grande di San Marco** was once the richest Venetian confraternity. It retains its trompe l'oeil Renaissance façade, assembly rooms and chapter house.
SEE ALSO CHURCHES, P.41; SCUOLE P.118–9

Arsenale

Founded in 1104, this military complex became Europe's largest medieval shipyard. A church has stood on the remote island since 775; the current **San Pietro di Castello** was constructed to a design by Palladio and was the city cathedral until 1807.
SEE ALSO CHURCHES, P.42; MONUMENTS, P.72

oldest ethnic communities in Venice and the church is still used as their place of worship. San Giovanni in Bragora is a treasured, late Gothic parish church. The interior is notable for its Renaissance works of art.

The tiny *scuola* (confraternity) of **San Giorgio degli Schiavoni** founded by the Dalmatians and decorated with a vibrant pictorial cycle by Carpaccio. An architectural milestone, the church of **San Francesco della Vigna** was Sansovino's first creation in Venice and the first flowering of the High Renaissance in the city. The façade was added by Palladio.
SEE ALSO CHURCHES, P.39, 41; SCUOLE, P.119

Campo Santa Maria Formosa

A lovely asymmetrical space dotted with fruit and vegetable stalls and flanked by *palazzi* and open-air cafés.

The square used to provide a backdrop for traditional festivities, from masked balls to bear-baiting. The nearby **Fondazione Querini-Stampalia** comprises a delightful small gallery of Venetian paintings, a library, garden and café.
SEE ALSO MUSEUMS AND GALLERIES, P.79–80

Campo Santi Giovanni e Paolo

One of the most monumental squares in the whole of Venice, overlooked by a mag-

Below: intricate artwork is often overhead.

Cannaregio

This faded, northerly district, once the most fashionable in Venice, is a moody backwater and the site of the world's first Jewish ghetto. It is an ancient quarter that remains a bridge between Venice and the mainland, between the historic city and modernity. Cannaregio is a district for those who have tired of the monumental sites around San Marco. Walks in the melancholic neighbourhood at the edge of the city trace a landscape of peeling facades and humble workshops, broad canals and wind-buffeted quays. Northern Cannaregio, and notably the peaceful Madonna dell'Orto quarter, is one of the loveliest, but least explored parts of the city.

See Atlas Pages 134-135

0   200m

The Northern Quays

Madonna dell'Orto

Set on a harmonious square of herringbone design, the church is named after a miracle-working statue of the Madonna found in a nearby vegetable garden (*orto*). The quirky campanile is topped by an onion-shaped cupola. This was Tintoretto's parish church and is decorated with works he created *in situ*. He is buried here in a side chapel.
SEE ALSO CHURCHES, P.42–3

Campo dei Mori

The Moorish name derives from the Fondaco degli Arabi, the Arab trading centre that once stood here. The Gothic **Palazzo Mastelli** has a filigree balcony and a relief of a laden camel, lending the palace an Eastern flavour. The owners were Levantine merchants

Above: turbaned figure in the Campo dei Mori.

whose origins are alluded to in the Romanesque reliefs of turbaned Moors on the eastern side of the square.

Ponte della Sacca

This bridge looks out over the northern lagoon and San

Michele, island of the dead. At twilight, especially, this is a poignant place.

Campo dei Gesuiti

The square, on which the **Gesuiti** church and the **Oratorio dei Crociferi** both stand, is dotted with houses associated with guilds; on the walls are symbols or inscriptions referring to coopers, tailors and weavers. Just north of the square you can enjoy fine lagoon views from the Fondamenta Nuove.

The Gesuiti church is often confused with the Gesuati, in Dorsoduro, the other major Jesuit foundation in Venice. After their banishment was revoked, the Jesuits returned to Venice, and, in 1715 rebuilt this church, which is still run by the Order.
SEE ALSO CHURCHES, P.42

Santa Maria dei Miracoli

Within a maze of alleyways and canals, this lovely church seems to rise from the water. Perfect proportions make this a Renaissance miracle in miniature, gleaming with a soft marble sheen. Even the renowned John Ruskin, no fan of the Renaissance, was forced to admit the Miracoli to be 'the best possible

Left: Santa Maria dei Miracoli.

reveal lavish interiors, often with a Levantine feel. Gilt and stucco are used rather than marble, which was a material forbidden to Jews by the Venetians.

Ponte delle Guglie

The charming stone and brick 'Bridge of the Obelisks' spans the Canale di Cannaregio, which was the main entrance to the city before the construction of the rail causeway in 1846. Gargoyles decorate the bridge's arch.

Palazzo Labia

Over the bridge, with outlooks on to both the Grand Canal and the Cannaregio Canal, the Baroque palace was built at the beginning of the 18th century by the fabulously rich Labia family who bought their way into Venetian nobility. Today it is the regional headquarters of RAI, Italian state television. Little known outside Italy, the ballroom boasts some splendid Tiepolo frescoes, with stunning decorative works in trompe l'oeil by Gerolama Mengozzi-Colonna.

SEE ALSO PALAZZI, P.101

Close to Campo dei Mori, the insignificant-looking house at no. 3399 Fondamenta dei Mori was the great Tintoretto's home from 1574 until his death in 1594.

example of a bad style'.

SEE ALSO CHURCHES, P.42

San Giovanni Crisostomo

This Renaissance terracotta-coloured church was the last work of Mauro Coducci. The marble interior contains a delightful altarpiece by Giovanni Bellini (1515), possibly also his last work.

Sandwiched between the canals of Rio San Giovanni Crisostomo and Rio del Fontego Tedeschi is the **Corte Seconda del Milion**, a little courtyard where Marco Polo reputedly lived. His house burnt down in 1596, but the well-head remains.

SEE ALSO CHURCHES, PAGE 43

The Venetian Ghetto

The **Campo del Ghetto Nuovo** is at the heart of the world's oldest ghetto, a fortified island created in 1516. Three of Venice's five remaining synagogues are set around the square. Although hidden behind nondescript façades, the synagogues

Below: signs and symbols in the Jewish Ghetto.

San Polo

San Polo curves into the left bank of the Grand Canal. The hub is the Rialto, 'the marketplace of the morning and evening lands', in Goethe's poetic evocation. The labyrinthine Rialto, with dark alleys and tiny squares, makes a sharp contrast to the open spaces around Campo San Polo. As the oldest district, the Rialto has the greatest number of Veneto-Byzantine palaces – many of these are covered in the Canale Grande chapter. San Polo is also home to two of the city's greatest sights: the Frari, a huge Franciscan church containing masterpieces by Titian and Bellini, and the Scuola Grande di San Rocco, a shrine to Tintoretto.

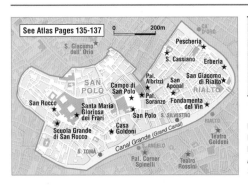

'What's new on the Rialto?' was Antonio's cry in Shakespeare's *The Merchant of Venice*. Gossip remains a popular Venetian pastime, and the Rialto is still a talking shop.

The **Pescheria** is the Rialto's lively fish market. Enjoy the bustle and have lunch in a *bacaro (see box below, right)*.
SEE ALSO FOOD, P.55

The Rialto

With a name derived from *rivus altus* (high bank), this was the first settlement of central Venice. The old mercantile district remains a hive of commercial activity, with a vibrant atmosphere, and has the greatest number of Veneto-Byzantine palaces.

Markets

The **Erberia** is the fruit and vegetable market overlooking the Grand Canal. Brightly painted boats from the lagoon supply the main markets with produce. Close by is the watergate, the 'tradesmen's entrance'. The profusion of herbs, flowers, fruit, and vegetables is a true delight.

San Giacomo di Rialto

Nestling comfortably among the fruit and vegetable stalls, the church is linked to St James, patron saint of goldsmiths and pilgrims. Both were much in evidence in the Rialto, even if the pilgrims were often in search of gold rather than God. This is reputedly the oldest church in Venice.
SEE ALSO CHURCHES, P.43

Fondamenta del Vin
Barrels of wine used to be unloaded on this quayside. It is now overrun by tempting but touristy trattorias and souvenir stalls. Facing it is the Riva del Ferro, where German barges once unloaded iron.

Left: brightly painted boats supply fish and produce to the Rialto markets.

Left: water taxi at the Rialto.

Campo San Polo

Lying at the heart of the San Polo quarter, this is the largest Venetian square after Piazza San Marco. Historically, this amphitheatre was the scene of bull-baiting, tournaments and processions, even a great 'bonfire of the vanities' in 1450. Today it is a popular venue for film screenings and carnival balls.

In the south-west corner of square is the Gothic **church of San Polo**. A 17th-century plaque outside the church forbids games, shopping and swearing 'on pain of prison, the galleys or exile'.
SEE ALSO CHURCHES, P.43

> The Rialto market is the ideal place to indulge in a Venetian bar crawl, a *giro di ombre*, in the traditional bars known as *bacari*. They are among the oldest in Venice, some dating back to the 15th century, *(see Bars and Cafés, p.33)*.

Casa Goldoni

The birthplace of the prolific Venetian playwright, Carlo Goldoni (1707-93), nowadays regarded as one of the finest European dramatists. His plays make skillful use of the Venetian language. The house has an interesting collection of theatrical memorabilia.
SEE ALSO PALAZZI, PAGE 100

The Frari

Officially known as **Santa Maria Gloriosa dei Frari**, this, along with San Giovanni e Paolo *(see p.41)*, is the largest of all Venetian Gothic churches. The hulking Franciscan complex, founded in the 13th century, was rebuilt in the 14th and 15th centuries. As much a gallery as a church, the Frari houses two of Titian's masterpieces, and works of art by Giovanni Bellini, Donatello and Vivarini.
SEE ALSO CHURCHES, P.43

Scuola Grande di San Rocco

One of the greatest city sights, San Rocco is the grandest of the *scuole* and acts as a venue for Baroque recitals. The society is dedicated to St Roch, the French saint of plague victims, who so impressed the Venetians that they stole his relics and canonised him. The 16th-century building is also a shrine to Tintoretto, the great Mannerist painter, whose pictorial cycle adorns the walls.
SEE ALSO SCUOLE, P.120-1

San Rocco

Tucked into a tiny square between the *scuola* and the Frari, this little church was begun in 1489 and restored in the 18th century. Its gloomy interior is lined with works by Tintoretto and Il Pordenone, another Mannerist painter. The 1911 Britannica states that 'so far as mere flesh-painting is concerned he was barely inferior to Titian in breadth, pulpiness and tone'.

Below: The Glory of St Roch.

17

Santa Croce

San Polo's sister *sestiere* is the least known district of the city. Fine palaces line the northern arc of the Grand Canal (many of these are covered in the Canale Grande chapter), but the heart of Sant Croce consists of a warren of alleys, lined by tall, tightly-packed houses and peaceful squares where local life carries on undisturbed by tourism. It offers many daytime attractions, but is also a delightful area to go for an evening stroll, its quiet streets interspersed with lively squares dotted with neighbourhood bars, pizzerias and trattorias. The hub, Campo San Giacomo dell' Orio, comes alive in the early evening.

San Stae

Overlooking the Grand Canal San Stae (an abbreviation for Saint Eustachius) is closer to Palladian in style than Baroque, with Corinthian columns set on high plinths. The richly decorated church was built in the early 18th century and over-restored in 1977-8.

Palazzo Mocenigo

Not to be confused with the Ca; Mocenigo on the Grand Canal, this well-preserved palace gives you a rare insight into 18th-century Venetian living. Rooms are lavishly decorated with fres-

See Atlas Pages 134-136

coed ceilings, gilded furnishings and Murano chandeliers. The Mocenigos were among the oldest and most illustrious of Venetian families, producing seven doges. Palazzo Mocenigo also houses a museum of antique textiles and costumes.
SEE ALSO PALAZZI, P.101

Campo di Santa Maria Mater Domini

This harmonious square is hemmed in by medieval palaces and a fashionable bar. Set back from the square is the equally beguiling Renaissance church of **Santa Maria Mater Domini**, with fine 16th-century paintings, including one by Tintoretto.

San Giacomo dell'Orio

Tucked into a corner of a leafy square of the same

name, this church has an inviting Romanesque atmosphere lit by diffuse light. The coherence is remarkable given the eclectic nature of the church, which spans many centuries since its 9th century foundation. A stroll around the building reveals the characteristic bulbous apses, and is an invitation to linger in a bar on one of the city's most captivating squares.
SEE ALSO CHURCHES, P.43

The stretch of the Grand Canal from the train station to the Rialto Bridge is lined by historic warehouses and palaces, including Veneto-Byzantine gems. Most of these can only be appreciated from the water. *See also Canale Grande, p.10–11.*

Below: stopping for a chat.

Left: Ponte dei Frari.

The *scuole* were charitable lay associations. Until the fall of the Republic (in 1797) they acted as a state within a state, looking after members' spiritual, moral and material welfare. Each of the organisations decorated their buildings with lavish works by leading artists. Today several of the *scuole*, including San Giovanni Evangelista, make fine settings for classical concerts. *See also Scuole, p.118–21*

Giardini Papadopoli

To the northwest of the *sestiere* lie the Papadopoli Gardens. This green space, formerly a botanical garden attached to a palace of the same name, was created to resemble an English park. It is smaller than it was, as part of it was incorporated into the Piazzale Roma when the Rio Nuovo was opened in 1933.

Piazzale Roma

This unattractive square may be your first view of Venice if you arrive by bus or taxi from the airport, as it is linked to the mainland by a causeway.

Scuola Grande di San Giovanni Evangelista

The distinctive Renaissance marble portal and courtyard of this scuola is watched over by an eagle, the symbol of St John, the confraternity's patron saint. The ideal way to see the interior is to attend a concert, but visits can also be made by appointment (tel: 041-718 234). Opposite is a minor 15th-century church of the same name (it means St John the Evangelist).

SEE ALSO SCUOLE, P.120

Below: Campo di San Giacomo dell'Orio.

Dorsoduro

The name simply means 'hard back', so called because the district occupies the largest area of firm land in Venice. This is the smartest residential area of Venice, a great place for walking, and a haven for wealthy expatriates. It stretches from La Salute, the monumental church guarding the entrance to the Grand Canal, to the Rio Nuovo-Rio Foscari in the west. The eastern section, which is the most picturesque, is home to two of the city's finest art collections and the southern spur of the Zattere makes the most enchanting Venetian promenade. Campo Santa Margherita, to the north, is a cheerful district of shopkeepers, students and arty types.

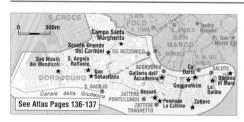

See Atlas Pages 136-137

Arguably the best gelateria in Venice is in Dorsoduro: **Nico**, at Zattere 922. The Venetian ice-cream speciality is *gianduiotto*, an indulgent blend of hazelnuts, chocolate and whipped cream.

La Salute

Eastern Dorsoduro is dominated by this Baroque basilica. It was built in thanks–giving for delivery from a 1630 plague. The interior is rather solemn, the exterior more joyous, with the majestic dome dominating the skyline.
SEE ALSO CHURCHES, P.44

The Zattere

This broad sunny promenade stretches all the way along Dorsoduro's southern shore, flanked by cafés, churches, boathouses and warehouses. Created in 1516, it was named after the cargoes of wood that were unloaded here (*zattere* means floating rafts). This is the Venetians' favourite walking place.

Dogana di Mare

Occupying the triangular tip of Dorsoduro this was the customs house where ships' cargoes were inspected before dropping anchor in front of the Doge's Palace. It is undergo-

Above: Punta della Dogana.

ing restoration to become a gallery of modern art.
SEE ALSO MONUMENTS, P.73

Magazzini del Sale

The former salt warehouses double as an exhibition space during the Biennale art festival.
SEE ALSO MONUMENTS, P.73

Pensione La Calcina

On the Zattere, this is also known as Ruskin's House.

The art historian stayed here when it was an inn frequented by artists. Today it is a popular hotel with an enviable setting.
SEE ALSO BARS AND CAFÉS, P.35; HOTELS, P.63

Gesuati

This grandiose church on the Zattere is a supreme example of 18th-century Venetian architecture, not to be confused with the Gesuiti in Cannaregio.
SEE ALSO CHURCHES, P.44

Squero di San Trovaso

A picturesque gondola repair-yard on the Rio di San Trovaso, one of only four surviving *squeri* in Venice.
SEE ALSO MONUMENTS, P.73

Along the Grand Canal

Ca' Dario

A beautiful Gothic palace said to be cursed because tragedy has befallen successive owners over the course of five centuries.
SEE ALSO PALAZZI, PAGE 100

Peggy Guggenheim Collection

The gallery in the Palazzo

Left: La Salute.

San Nicolò dei Mendicoli

In a dilapidated district in western Dorsoduro, this former fishermen's church is surprisingly sumptuous. Sensitively restored by Venice in Peril in the 1970s it has a squat Romanesque bell tower and a brick facade lit by mullioned windows.
SEE ALSO CHURCHES, P.44

Scuola Grande dei Carmini

The headquarters of the Carmelite confraternity. The uninspired façade conceals a lavish 18th-century interior, with an upper hall decorated by Tiepolo. The *scuola* was built next to the Carmelite church, Santa Maria dei Carmini, also known as Santa Maria del Carmelo.
SEE ALSO SCUOLE, P.121

> The Ponte dei Pugni (Bridge of Fists) between San Barnaba and Santa Margherita gets its name from the factional brawls between rival clans that took place here. The fights were banned in 1705.

Venier dei Leoni contains a superb collection of modern art, featuring Chagall, Kandinsky, Picasso and others.
SEE ALSO MUSEUMS AND GALLERIES, P.78–9

Galleria dell'Accademia

Housed in La Carità, a complex of church and convent, the Accademia gallery is home to the world's greatest collection of Venetian art.
SEE ALSO MUSEUMS AND GALLERIES, P.81–2

West Dorsoduro

San Sebastiano

An early 16th-century church, adorned with Veronese's opulent masterpieces. It is praised as a perfect marriage of the arts, with architecture, painting and sculpture in perfect harmony.
SEE ALSO CHURCHES, P.44

Angelo Raffaele

This ancient church was reconstructed in 1618. The story of Tobias and his guardian angel Raffaele is recounted on the panel paintings over the organ loft.

Campo Santa Margherita

The liveliest square in the whole district with an increasing number of late-opening bars. At one end is the free-standing **Scuola dei Varotari**, formerly the tanners' guild. Another side of the square is bordered by dignified palaces with overhanging roofs.

Below: 18th-century pulpit in the church of Angelo Raffaele.

Giudecca and San Giorgio Maggiore Islands

Giudecca is the most contradictory of Venetian islands, home to the city's most luxurious hotel and its most raffish district. This used to be a depressed island of decaying tenements, but it is undergoing a rebirth, with the restoration of landmark buildings, and the conversion of an old flour mill and furniture factories into a grand hotel and luxury apartments. The island of San Giorgio Maggiore, shaded by cypress trees, is famous for its great Benedictine complex and still has a secluded air.

Giudecca

Il Redentore

A Venetian landmark, visible from every side of St Mark's Basin, the graceful Church of the Redeemer was built in thanksgiving for the end of a devastating plague in 1576. Designed as a votive temple, it is still the scene of Venice's most beguiling summer festival. Architectural purists feel that this Palladian master-piece, inspired by the Pantheon in Rome, surpasses even San Giorgio.
SEE ALSO CHURCHES, P.45

The Garden of Eden

This exotic garden, close to Il Redentore, is named after the Englishman who created it, not the biblical paradise. Facing the garden is the former English Hospital, which cared for impecunious British expatriates in Edwardian times.

Le Zitelle

The complex bears the Palladian hallmarks of stylistic

Above: San Giorgio Maggiore.

unity, coherent classicism and an inspired sense of proportion. In keeping with Venetian tradition, it was originally designed as a convent but became a noted musical conservatoire. The complex is now a convention centre, making access difficult. Many visitors end up in Cip's Club, the elegant waterfront bar

which lies just beyond the convent.

Hotel Cipriani

Set on the eastern spit of the island, this is one of the world's most exclusive hotels. Cipriani's liveried motor boats ferry guests across from San Marco to this oasis of peace. The hotel incorporates a Gothic palace and has lush gardens full of azaleas, rhododen-drons and oleanders framing the wide expanse of the swimming pool.
SEE ALSO HOTELS, P.65

Sant' Eufemia

This building faces the great Gesuati church across the water on Dorsoduro. Marred by remodelling, it sur-vives as a bizarre mix of Veneto-Byzantine capitals, Rococo stuccowork and 18th-century paintings.

Molino Stucky

At the western end of the island looms the neo-Gothic

Left: San Giorgio Maggiore by night.

Tintoretto, and some fabulous wooden choir stalls. A lift whisks visitors to the top of the tower for fabulous views over the city and lagoon.
SEE ALSO CHURCHES, P.45

Fondazione Cini

The Benedictine monastery adjoining the church was rebuilt in the 13th century following an earthquake and later became a centre of learning. The Fondazione Cini was created by Count Vittorio Cini (1884–1977) as a memorial to his son, who died in a flying accident. The centre funds restoration projects and stages major exhibitions. Baroque architect Longhena designed the monastery's ceremonial double staircase and library, on the site of Michelozzi's Renaissance library; Palladio designed the Cloister of the Cypresses and the refectory. The open-air **Teatro Verde** has recently reopened as a venue for opera, surrounded by illuminated parkland, and with two bars beside the stage for refreshments.
SEE ALSO MUSEUMS AND GALLERIES, P.82; MUSIC, P.84–5

Elton John has a home on Giudecca, close to the Hotel Cipriani. Simplistic though it sounds, some local people credit him with turning the tide in what was a resolutely un-glitzy island.

Molino Stucky, a former grain silo, pasta factory and flour mill. It was built in 1895 by the Swiss merchant, Giovanni Stucky, who was murdered by one of his workers in 1910. After decades of neglect, and arson in 2003, this fortress-like building has been converted into a luxury of Hilton hotel with the largest congress centre in Venice.
SEE ALSO HOTELS, P.65

Island of San Giorgio Maggiore

Church of San Giorgio Maggiore

A familiar landmark seen from San Marco, the majestic church with its lofty cam-
panile and brilliantly white façade appears suspended in the inner lagoon. Built between 1559–80 the complex is among Palladio's greatest architectural achievements and, like Il Redentore, it is unsurpassed in its cool, rational, classical beauty. The interior houses two late masterpieces by

Below: converted flour mill, now the Hilton Molino Stucky.

23

Murano and Burano

Murano is proud of its reputation as a highly celebrated glass-making centre and an 18th-century summer resort for the nobility. The majority of visitors are enticed by the glass-making, and commercialism rules here, although an impressive Byzantine church and cluster of bars add to the island's appeal. Burano, the home of fishermen and lace-makers, is the most vibrant of the Venetian islands, a splash of colour in a bleak lagoon, dispelling any mournfulness with its parade of colourful fishermen's cottages. Both islands can be reached by frequent ferries which depart from the Fondamenta Nuove in northern Venice.

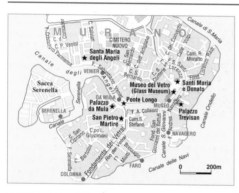

Da Romano, a seafood restaurant on Burano's Via Baldassare Galuppi, is one of those canny places where previous owners accepted paintings as payment for meals. The subsequent collection is a good one. *See also Restaurants, p.115.*

las to priceless chandeliers. For the quality glass you should always try bargaining. SEE ALSO SHOPPING, P.123–5

San Pietro Martire

Towards the end of the Fondamenta dei Vetrai, you come to San Pietro Martire. This Gothic church has a Renaissance portal and a richly-coloured altarpiece by Giovanni Bellini (1488), depicting Doge Agostino Barbarigo being presented to the Virgin.

Palazzo da Mula

Further down the quayside this Gothic palace with a Byzantine walled garden is home to a glassworks. From here, there is a lovely view west along Canale degli Angeli to the abandoned church of Santa Maria degli Angeli. SEE ALSO PALAZZI, P.101

Museo del Vetro

The Glass Museum, within the 17th-century palazzo Giustinian, contains a stunning collection of antique pieces, from

Murano

Fondamenta dei Vetrai

This is the heart of the glass-making district, where showrooms along the quayside offer a chance to admire the glass-blowers' skills. There is no obligation to buy and you can watch the craftsmen blow a blob of molten glass, and with a spatula or pincers, twist, turn, pinch and flatten it into the perfect shape of an animal or bird. Shops along the quayside here sell everything from mini glass gondo-

Left: Fondamenta dei Vetrai.

Genuine hand-made Burano-point lace is ridiculously expensive, but that is to be expected as it takes 10 women up to three years to make a single tablecloth.

Venice led to the inevitable decline of the industry but a revival took place in 1872 when a lacemaking school was founded here to combat local poverty. Most pieces on display in the museum date from the 19th century. Lace-making courses are held here and you can occasionally still see local women busily knotting away in the old tradition.
SEE ALSO MUSEUMS AND GALLERIES, P.82

San Martino
The 16th-century church, on the same piazza as the Museo del Merletto, can be spotted from afar by its acutely tilting tower. Works of art within the church include a *Crucifixion* by Tiepolo.

Mazzorbo
Cross the footbridge to this backwater of orchards and gardens. The salt marshes and mudflats are being reinstated to restore the lagoon's ecological balance and act as a sea defence against high tides and storms.

Roman times to the 18th century. The classical **Palazzo Trevisan**, with an interior frescoed by Veronese, faces the Glass Museum.
SEE ALSO MUSEUMS AND GALLERIES, P. 82; PALAZZI, P.101

Santi Maria e Donato
The finest church on Murano. Founded in the 7th-century, it was rebuilt in Veneto-Byzantine style, and is graced by a 12th-century apse decorated with blind arches and loggias. The charm of the interior has survived much tampering, with a Gothic ship's-keel ceiling, marble columns and Veneto-Byzantine capitals.
SEE ALSO CHURCHES, P.45

Burano
Via Galuppi
The main street of Burano is lined with fishermen's cottages. Tradition has it that the houses were painted different colours to enable fishermen to recognise their homes from

the sea. Their wives painted the family homes in bold colours, often adding geometrical motifs over the doorways. The street is lined with lace shops and traditional trattorias, the places for the best crab and squid dishes.

Museo del Merletto
The lace museum, which was formerly the Burano lace school, is on the main Piazza Baldassare Galuppi. The downfall of the Republic of

Below: modern and affordable Murano glassware.

The Lido

This long strip of land, lying between the city and the Adriatic, belongs neither to Venice nor the mainland. This reflects the Lido's prime function, to protect Venice from the engulfing tides. In spirit, it is a place apart, not quite a traditional summer resort nor a residential suburb. There is a touch of unreality about the Lido, hence its role as a superior film-set. In this faded fantasy, neo-Gothic piles vie with Art Nouveau villas and a mock-Moorish castle. Although most day-trippers stray no further than the beaches and smart hotels, the Lido offers more subtle pleasure from its belle époque architecture to a gentle cycle ride along the sea walls.

Gran Viale Santa Maria Elisabetta

The ferries from San Marco deposit visitors among the traffic close to the Gran Viale, the main shopping street that cuts across the island from the lagoon shore to the Adriatic. An air of gracious living still permeates the broad, busy avenue. The Viale ends with the domes and ramps of the Blue Moon, a new public beach pavilion with a pier, restaurant, bar and terraces looking over the sea.

The 16th-century church, **Santa Maria Elisabetta**, stands close to the jetties where you disembark from the ferries.

> The Lido is Thomas Mann's Venice, a place of decadence and spiritual dislocation. To many people, it is known mainly as the setting for the moody 1970 film, *Death in Venice. See also Film, p.52–3.*

Above: Hôtel des Bains.

Lungomare

The seafront promenade, reached via the Gran Viale, is the focus of the summer evening *passeggiata*, when people wander up and down greeting friends. Beyond lie the best Adriatic beaches, private pockets of sand bedecked with colourful cabins.

Hôtel des Bains

Thomas Mann's stay in this elegant, ecletic Edwardian palace helped inspire his evocative novella, *Death in Venice*. To Mann, even the beach spelt foreboding: 'Evening too was rarely lovely, balsamic with the breath of flowers and shrubs from the nearby park.' The hotel retains an air of grandeur and finds favour with stars.

SEE ALSO HOTELS, P.65

Hotel Westin Excelsior

Another famous Lido landmark, the Excelsior is an exuberant piece of late 19th/early 20th century neo-Byzantine architecture, reminiscent of a Moorish castle.

Palazzo del Cinema

Standing at the grander end of the seafront, this is typical of the functionalist buildings of the Fascist era, and is now renowned as the focus of the **Venice Film Festival** each September. Built in 1937, the Palazzo has been the Festi-

Right: Lido di Venezia.

Left: sunbathing on Excelsior beach, 1954.

Book lagoon visits with nature and archaeology specialists, **Natura Venezia** (www.natura-venezia.it). **Rivivinatura** (www.rivivinatura.it) also run environmental tours and excursions.

monastery, where the doge prayed after the Marriage of the Sea ceremony, held on Ascension Day. From here, there is a clear view of the Fortezza di Sant'Andrea on the island of Le Vignole, the impressive bastion that defended the lagoon.

Spiaggia Comunale

This is a somewhat scruffy public beach at the east end of the island. If you fancy swimming (and stories of pollution don't seem to deter the crowds), bear in mind that most of the other beaches are privately owned and charge a fee.

Pellestrina

This very narrow strip of land is bounded by the *murazzi*, the sea walls that protect the lagoon city. For the first time since the city's creation, the sea defences are being radically re-thought to prevent *aqua alta* and a mobile dam is being built nearby.

SEE ALSO ENVIRONMENT, P.46–7

val's main home for 60 years. The Venice Film Festival is the world's oldest, and now rivals Cannes in prestige, with fans claiming it out-shines the Côte d'Azur in terms of glitz and glamour.
SEE ALSO FILM, P.52; FESTIVALS, P.51

Malamocco

This was the site of the first capital of the lagoon before it was engulfed by a tidal wave. There are no traces left of the 8th-century capital, but this fishing village has several

seafood restaurants and a bell tower recalling the campanile of San Marco. The spit eventually peters out in the sand dunes of Alberoni.

The Eastern End

Nuovo Cimitero Israelitico

The Jewish cemetery, lies on Via Cipro, the street cutting across the island. It dates back to 1386 and reflects the special status of the Jewish community in Venice.

San Nicolò

A church and Benedictine

Architecture

The wealth of the city's architecture reflects a remarkable diversity of traditions and influences. The palaces flanking the Grand Canal span some 500 years, from Veneto-Byzantine to Palladian; but the essence of Venetian architecture resides most eloquently in the palaces built in the distinctive Venetian-Gothic style. The end of the Venetian Republic in 1797 more or less spelt the end of the evolving architecture; and in recent times lack of space combined with Venetian conservatism has precluded the construction of any great deal of modern architecture.

The Byzantine

The Byzantine-style **Santa Maria dell'Assunta** basilica on Torcello island was founded in AD639 *(see p.45)*. The 12th and 13th centuries saw the rise of private palazzi in the Veneto-Byzantine style: an oriental, flowery form, with ornate capitals, pediments and niches and Byzantine arches. Slender columns and stilted arches gave way to Moorish design, especially the horseshoe arch and the inflected arch, resembling a quivering flame.

The **Ca' da Mosto** on the Grand Canal is a fine example *(see p.97)*. The Veneto-Byzantine style influenced palaces and warehouses *(fondaci)* well into the 14th-century. The model was the *casa-fondaco*, combining the roles of commercial office and family home. The Fondaco dei Tedeschi on the Grand Canal is a good example.

Venetian Gothic (13th to mid-15th Centuries)

Gothic is the most common city style. The pure curve of a Byzantine arch progressed

Above: the arcaded staircase of the Contarini-Bovolo palace.

to a pointed Moorish arch and then to a Gothic ogival arch. Glorious windows were framed by filigree stonework, with brick and stucco used in delicate two-tone colour combinations. The **Ca' d'Oro** is arguably the finest Gothic palace, decorated in a Venetian interpretation of the Flamboyant Gothic style, with stone tracery that

becomes more fragile as it reaches the top *(see p.97)*. The **Frari** is the most glorious of Venetian-Gothic churches, based on a Latin cross plan with three aisles and a cross-vaulted roof *(see p.43)*.

Early Renaissance (Second Half of the 15th Century)

The 15th century was a golden age for all Venetian art forms. 1460 saw the construction of the ceremonial Arsenale gateway, by Antonio Gambello, considered the first flowering of Renaissance architecture in Venice. Mauro Coducci (c.1440–1504) introduced Tuscan sophistication to Gothic Venice. His earliest creation was San Michele in Isola (1468-77), the first Renaissance church in Venice; he also designed the graceful upper façade of **San Zaccaria** *(see p.39)*. Another key structure of the period was the delightful church of **Santa Maria dei Miracoli** *(see p.42)* designed by master craftsmen Pietro Lombardo and sons.

Left: Palazzo Loredan, a fine Veneto-Byzantine palace.

or grotesque masks. The prime exponent of Venetian Baroque is Baldassare Longhena (1597–1682) who created the theatrical church of La Salute *(see p.44)*.

Classical Revival (18th Century)

A reaction against Baroque and a return to Palladian values. Grandiose palaces were designed with monumental staircases. Massari (1686–1766) was drawn to the new spirit of the Classical revival. He created the Palladian façade of the **Gesuati** church *(see p.44)* and his great masterpiece, the church of La Pietà *(see p.41)*.

Modern Venice

The 16th-century **campanile** in Piazza San Marco collapsed in 1902 and was rebuilt exactly as it was. In the 1930s the heavy iron **Accademia Bridge** was replaced by a wooden structure. In 1996 **La Fenice** was destroyed by fire, and it took 8 years to restore it to its former glory. Modern architecture is rare in Venice, but two major engineering projects are ongoing: the **Mose Dam** *(see p.46)* and the **Calatrava Bridge** *(see p.71)*.

The latest addition to the city is the Calatrava bridge across the Grand Canal. This slender steel structure makes a splash in a city as conservative as Venice.

The High Renaissance

The High Renaissance, the apogee of refinement, was led by Jacopo Sansovino (1486–1570). In his role as Superintendent of the Works, he had great influence over Venetian architecture. In Piazza San Marco he designed the Library and Mint; **Ca' Grande** *(see p.95–6)* on the Grand Canal is a magnificent Classical triumph. Here, as in other Venetian palaces, Sansovino established triple water-entrance arches and spandrels adorned with sculpture.

Palladianism

Andrea Palladio (1508–80) dedicated the end of his career to transforming the Venetian skyline with his bold buildings. His two masterpieces are the church of **San Giorgio Maggiore** (1565), a model of stylistic unity and coherent classicism *(see p.45)*;

and **Il Redentore** (1576), characterised by rigour and restraint, and inspired by the Pantheon in Rome *(see p.45)*.

Baroque (17th to 18th Centuries)

Baroque Venice belonged to a bold, yet less inspired age. By turns ponderous and whimsical, this was a relatively sober form of Baroque, tempered by Palladianism. The style is characterised by stone rustication, and revels in exuberant stucco work and flamboyant friezes, with every surface studded with garlands, cherubs, coats of arms

Below: intricate tracery of the Doge's Palace Gothic façade.

Bars and Cafés

There is no shortage of bars and cafés in Venice, from the opulent and expensive establishments in Piazza San Marco to the typically Venetian bacari, the traditional wine bars that serve *cichetti*, the local version of tapas. Some of the bacari are old-fashioned, unchanged in style for years; others have been renovated to attract a younger clientele. There are also, of course, many bars that cater to the tourist trade without making much effort at all, but in the less touristy parts of Venice you can find excellent osterias or trattorias serving a hearty workers' menu at midday at a very reasonable price.

Where to Find Them

The following selection of bars and cafés – it is difficult to distinguish between the two in Venice – are listed by area, starting with those around San Marco. Those that specialize in late nights can be found in the Nightlife section (*see p.87–9*), although there is some crossover between the two.

Below: Caffè Florian on St Mark's Square.

Piazza San Marco

Caffè Florian
Piazza San Marco; tel: 041-520 5641; closed Wed; vaporetto: San Marco-Vallaresso; map p.138 B2
The renowned Florian is the place for a prosecco or a Venetian spritz in style, while drowning in dubious musical offerings and watching children chasing pigeons in the square. You pay more when the band strikes up.

Caffè Quadri
Piazza San Marco; tel: 041-522 2105; closed Mon in winter; vaporetto: San Marco-Vallaresso; map p.138 B2
Close your ears to the rival quartet in Caffè Florian while you have a drink in the square or in an interior adorned with stuccowork, red damask and Murano chandeliers.

Sestiere San Marco

Alla Botte
Calle della Bissa, near Campo San Bartolomeo; tel: 041-520 9775; closed Sun D and Thur; vaporetto: Rialto; map p.138 B3
Although it is in the heart of the tourist area, Alla Botte

provides sound Venetian tapas in a rustic setting, and the service is efficient.

Bacaro Lounge
Salizzada San Moisè; tel: 041-296 0687; daily 10am–2am; vaporetto: San Marco-Vallaresso; map p.137 E3
A cool, cutting-edge wine and cocktail bar with bar snacks and light lunches (more elegant upstairs) and an adjoining ultra-trendy multi-media centre and bookshop.

Cavatappi
Campo della Guerra, near San Zulian; tel: 041-296 0252; closed Sun D and Mon; vaporetto: San Zaccaria or Rialto; map p.138 B2
A fashionable, contemporary-style wine bar serving good bar snacks and light lunches or smarter evening meals.

If you go to a bar for breakfast you will notice that for local people it is not a leisurely affair. Usually they swallow a coffee and grab a pastry while standing at the bar and the whole transaction is over in a flash.

Left: coffee served in splendour on Piazzetta San Marco.

Despite offering two-tier prices for Venetians and visitors, Vino Vino is still a rarity in the touristy opera-house area: a genuine, gruff and fusty all-day wine bar with a large selection of wines (there are said to be 350) sold by the glass or bottle.

Vitae
Salizzada San Luca; tel: 041-520 5205; closed Sat L and Sun; vaporetto: Rialto; map p.137 E3
This is a sleek wine bar catering to a young crowd, with tasty nibbles (*crostini* and *tramezzini*) at basic prices.

Al Volto
Calle Cavalli; tel: 041-522 8945; closed Sun; vaporetto: Rialto; map p.137 D4
This is an utterly unfashionable and unpretentious wine bar, its atmospheric interior lined with bottles. It serves decent *cichetti* (tapas) along with the huge selection of good wines.

Centrale
Piscina Frezzeria; tel: 041-296 0664; open daily 7pm–2am; €€; vaporetti: San Marco-Vallaresso; map p.138 A2
This futuristic, sleek bar-restaurant and music club feels more Milanese than Venetian. Set in a converted cinema, the 16th-century *palazzo* incorporates cutting-edge design. Sample a full Mediterranean menu or just snack while chilling out to contemporary sounds.

Harry's Bar
Calle Vallaresso; tel: 041-528 5777; daily, till late; vaporetto: San Marco-Vallaresso; map p.137 E3
The legendary bar and restaurant is a place you must visit at least once, and try a Bellini cocktail (the house speciality combining prosecco and peach juice), even if the price puts you off having a second. Despite its fame, it is a surprisingly unpretentious place.

Rosa Salva
Mercerie San Salvador; tel: 041 522 7934; daily; vaporetto: Rialto; map p.137 E4

A branch of the best-known Venetian *pasticceria*, where local people gather for a quick morning brioche and cappuccino or an afternoon pastry.

Vino Vino
Calle delle Veste; tel: 041-241 7688; closed Tue; vaporetto: Santa Maria del Giglio or San Marco-Vallaresso; map p.137 E2

Right: Vino Vino, San Marco.

Canale Grande

B Bar

Hotel Bauer, Campo San Moisè; tel: 041-520 7022; daily; vaporetto: San Marco-Valla-resso; map p.137 E2

This is celebrated locally as a trendy cocktail bar, popular with Venetians, thanks to its skilled barmen and the pleasure of drinking on the Grand Canal terrace.

Castello

Castello has fewer bars than other neighbourhoods; apart from those in the smart hotels that line Riva degli Schiavoni, which are best in the evening. A few to look out for are:

Florian Art Caffè

Fondazione Querini-Stampalia, Calle Querini; tel: 041-271 1411; closed Mon; vaporetto: San Zaccaria or Rialto; map p.138 C3

Set in this quirky gallery is the only other branch of San Marco's Caffè Florian *(see above)* and a peaceful place for coffee or a quick bite.

Rosa Salva

Campo Santi Giovanni e Paolo; tel: 041-522 7949; daily; vaporetto: Fondamenta Nuove; map p.134 A4

Another branch of the original and famous Venetian *pasticceria*, serving coffee, delicious pastries, cakes and ice creams at all hours of the day. The tables in the square are a lovely place to sit and watch the world go by.

Zanzibar

Campo Santa Maria Formosa; daily; vaporetto: Rialto or San Zaccaria p 138 C2

A lively canalside kiosk-bar, ideal for a lunchtime sandwich or a giant spritz, with an eclectic mixture of background music.

Cannaregio

Cannaregio tends to be a relatively cheap district for restaurants, many of which are just bars or basic inns; in those mentioned below, you can just have a drink or snack.

Most Venetian ice-cream bars – *gelaterie* – also serve coffee, which is a delicious accompaniment to the ice cream, and sometimes liqueurs as well. The best ices can be found in gelaterie on the Zattere.

Algiubagio

Fondamenta Nuove; tel: 041-523 6084; closed Wed; vaporetto: Fondamenta Nuove; map p.134 A4

Convenient for the vaporetto stop, this is a much-needed retreat from the windswept quaysides, and a chance for a coffee, liqueur, snack or full meal.

Anice Stellato

Fondamenta della Sensa; tel: 041-720 744; closed Mon–Tue; vaporetto: Guglie or Sant'Alvise; map p.134 C1

Always packed with local people who come for great value *cichetti* at the bar or full meals, by the canalside in summer.

La Cantina

Campo San Felice; tel: 041-522 8258; closed Sun and Mon; vaporetto: Ca' d'Oro; map p.135 D2

This is an old-style *bacaro* serving fine wines, soups, salami or cheese plates.

Fiddler's Elbow

Campo già Testori, near the Strada Nuova; tel: 041 523 9930; 5pm–1am daily; vaporetto: Ca' d'Oro; map p.135 D2

Venetian-run Irish pub popular with locals as well as tourists and ex-pats. Sporting events are show on the big screen.

Osteria al Bomba

Calle de l'Oca, close to Strada Nuova; tel: 041-520 5175; daily; vaporetto: Ca' d'Oro; map p.138 B1–A1

A traditional inn with a wide range of Venetian treats.

Vecia Carbonera

Rio Terrà della Maddalena, beside Ponte Sant'Antonio; tel:

Below: good views can be had from the Rialto Bridge cafés, but better *bacari* are found in the backstreets.

041-710 376; closed Mon; vaporetto: San Stae; map p.135 C3-D2

On the route to the station, this is a rustic-style wine bar with decent tapas and twice weekly jazz concerts.

San Polo

Al Bancogiro

Campo San Giacometto; tel: 041-523 2061; closed Sun evening and Mon; vaporetto: San Silvestro; map p.137 E4

A good place to end a Rialto bar crawl, in a bar that brings the *bacaro* concept up to date without betraying its rustic roots. Right by the market, it is an idiosyncratic, yet deservedly popular place. Eat and drink at an indoor bar or outside on the terrace in summer.

Ae Do Spade

Calle delle Do Spade, Rialto; tel: 041-521 0574; closed Wed in winter; vaporetto: San Silvestro; map p.137 E4

This place initially looks very touristy, but it is in fact popular with the Venetians. The signature dish is the spicy sandwich known as *paperini*. The service is prompt and friendly.

Da Elio

Campo delle Beccarie, close to the Rialto market; closed Mon; vaporetto: San Silvestro; map p.135 D1

Da Elio occupies a tiny corner of the fish market, where it sells delicate and unusual *cichetti* and wine.

Dei Frari

Campo dei Frari; tel: 041-524 1877; open daily; vaporetto: San Tomà; map p.137 C4

This is a boisterous bar serving a mainly young clientele with good tapas and cocktails.

Gelateria Millevoglie

Behind the Frari church; daily; vaporetto: San Tomà; map p.137 C4

Above: the stylish Centrale, *see p.31.*

Millevoglie has the reputation of being the area's best ice-cream bar – a good enough reason to seek it out on a sweltering day.

Da Pinto

Campo delle Beccarie; tel: 041-522 4599; closed Mon; vaporetto: San Silvestro; map p.135 D1

Although it also offers set menus Da Pinto is still popular with local people for tasty snacks such as *baccalà mantecato*, salami and bruschetta, all accompanied by simple Veneto wines, sold by the glass.

Ruga Rialto

Calle del Sturion, off Ruga Rialto; tel: 041-5211 243; daily 11am–3pm, 6pm–midnight; vaporetto: San Silvestro; map p.137 E4

A bohemian *bacaro* and inn with wooden benches, copper pots and simple but reliable dishes.

Santa Croce

Antico Dolo

Ruga Vecchia; tel: 041-522 6546; closed Sun; Vaporetto: San Silvestro; map p.137 E4

This is the place for the more unusual *cichetti*. It specialises in tripe and chicken gizzards, as well as the less controversial grilled peppers, and excellent bruschette topped with grilled vegetables or with *baccalà mantecato* (creamy cod paste).

Bagolo

Campo San Giacomo dell' Orio; tel: 041-717 584; closed Mon; Vaporetto: San Stae; map p.134 C1

This is a striking designer bar offering an array of salami and cold meats, fine wines and powerful grappas.

Easy Bar

Campo Santa Maria Mater Domini; daily; vaporetto: San Stae; map p.135 C1

Above: bar on Campo di Santa Margherita, the liveliest square in Dorsoduro.

The Easy Bar is an arty fusion of high-tech styling and old-fashioned brickwork, and is equally popular with local people and visitors.

Do Mori
Calle de Do Mori, off Ruga Vecchia; tel: 041-522 5401; closed Sun; vaporetto: San Silvestro; map p.137 E3

This quaint, rough-and-ready bar offers standing room only in which to enjoy its good wines and *tramezzini* (small triangular sandwiches with generous fillings).

Ai Vecio Fritoin
Calle della Regina; tel: 041-522 2881; closed Mon; vaporetto: San Stae; map p.135 D1

A *fritoin* is actually a stall or kiosk that serves take-away fried fish, but here you can enjoy it at the bar or table with a drink (full meals also available).

As is usual in most bars in Europe, you pay more if you sit at a table than if you stand at the bar, and you pay more if you sit outside on a terrace or at sidewalk tables than if you choose to sit inside.

Dorsoduro

Numerous bars are to be found in and around Campo Santa Margherita. Many come alive at night *(see Nightlife p.88 for further recommendations)*, but they are generally pleasant – and quieter – places to visit during the day as well. A few other, daytime bars are listed below.

Arca
Calle Lunga San Pantalon; tel: 041-524 2236; closed Sun; vaporetto: San Tomà; map p.136 C3

Arca has an excellent *cichetteria* (traditional tapas bar) located in front of the main trattoria and pizzeria. Open until midnight.

Cantinone già Schiavi
Fondamenta Nani; tel: 041-523 0034; Mon–Sat until 9pm vaporetto: Zattere ; map p.136 C2

Also known as Al Bottegon, this old-fashioned *enoteca*-bar is a popular local haunt, but tourists don't feel out of place. Good snacks – hams, salami and cheese.

Al Chioschetto
Fondamenta Zattere (by Capitaneria di Porto); tel: 338 117 4077; vaporetto: Zattere; map p.138 B1

A waterfront kiosk-bar that serves tasty snack lunches and is a great place for sunset aperitifs.

Enoteca San Barnaba
Calle Lunga San Barnaba; tel: 041-521 2754; closed Thur L and Wed; vaporetto: Ca' Rezzonico or San Basilio; map p.136 B2

This is a rustic-style inn where you can try regional wines and a selection of meaty bar snacks from the Friuli region.

Gobbetti
Rio Terrà Canal; vaporetto: Ca' Rezzonico; map p.136 C4

A tiny *pasticceria* producing mouth-watering cakes, *tiramisù*, chocolate mousse, and other calorie-loaded delights. Especially noted for noted for *la bomba,* a rich chocolaty tart.

Imagina
Rio Terrà Canal; tel: 041-241 0625; Mon–Sat 8am–2am; vaporetto: Ca' Rezzonico; map p.136 B3

Imagina is a buzzing New York-style designer bar and gallery whose offerings run the gamut from cappuccino

Below: Caffè Rosso, Campo di Santa Margherita.

Above: neighbourhood cafés.

Japanese-managed but Italian Futurist in conception, and modern Italian in its cuisine.

Suzie Café
Campo San Basilio; tel: 041-522 7502; closed Sun; vaporetto: San Basilio; map p.136 B2
Suzie Café is a studenty place that's good for drinks, light lunches and live music in summer, when it's lively at night.

Giudecca

Alla Palanca
Fondamenta del Ponte Piccolo; tel: 041-528 7719; Mon–Sat 7am–8.30pm; vaporetto: Palanca; map p.22
Welcoming bar/restaurant on the Giudecca waterfront, with lovely views of Dorsoduro.

The Lido

Trento
Via Sandro Gallo; tel: 041 526 5960; Mon–Sat 7am–9pm, 11pm in summer; vaporetti: Lido; map p.26
Locals flock to this excellent value bar/osteria at lunchtime for Venetian specialities such as baby octopus, *cotechino* (pork sausage) and salted dried cod.

and brioche to prosecco and late-night bar snacks.

SEE ALSO NIGHTLIFE P.88

Linea d'Ombra
Ponte dell'Umiltà, Zattere; tel: 041-520 4720; closed Wed; vaporetto: Salute map p.137 E2
A pleasing combination of a chic restaurant and an atmospheric waterfront bar, ideal for drinks, lunch or just an ice cream on the floating terrace.

Peggy Guggenheim Museum Café
Palazzo Venier dei Leoni, San Gregorio; tel: 041-240 5411; Wed–Mon 10am–6pm; vaporetto: Salute; map p.137 E2
The cool café inside the museum is the smartest gallery eatery in town, and ideal for snacks or light lunches when you've finished admiring the collection.

La Piscina
Pensione Calcina, Fondamenta Zattereai Gesuati; tel: 041-241 3889; closed Mon; vaporetto: Zattere; map p.137 C1
Come in the morning, afternoon or evening to enjoy teas, coffees and light Mediterranean dishes in this smart waterside café.

Paolin
Campo Santo Stefano; tel: 041-522 5576; closed Fri; vaporetto: Accademia; map p.137 D2
Just off the Grand Canal, Paolin is handy for the Accademia (over the bridge), and is famous for its delicious ice cream. The cocktails and bar snacks are pretty good, as well.

La Rivista
Rio Terrà Foscarini; tel: 041-240 1425; closed Mon; vaporetto: Accademia or Zattere; map p.137 B3
This stylish bar-restaurant is

Below: in a pinch, even hotels serve quality coffee.

Children

Venice may not be an obvious family destination, but it can be surprisingly rewarding. The waterways never fail to fascinate children of all ages, whether they are travelling on them or watching the canal traffic. In fine weather, a boat trip to the islands is a fun day out. It is also a city that makes wonderful ice-cream, and where pasta and pizza can be found in almost every restaurant. Added to this, Venetians, like most Italians, are indulgent towards children; and, if all else fails, there are wide, traffic-free squares with pigeons to chase and well-heads to clamber over.

Belltowers

For the most breathtaking views of the piazza and the city, take a lift to ascend the 100m of Venice's tallest building, the **Campanile di San Marco**. Or hop across to **San Giorgio Maggiore** on the island of the same name for equally stunning views from its belltower. Children usually love pointing out landmarks, vying to see who can spot the most.
SEE ALSO MONUMENTS, P.70; CHURCHES, P.45

Museums and Galleries

Museo Storico Navale
See p.80
For both children and adults the star attraction of the Naval History Museum is the model of the last Bucintoro, the gilded barge that was used by the doge on state occasions, although entire sections of other state barges and warships are also popular. There's also an annexe displaying a range of ships housed in the old naval sheds close to the Arsenale entrance.
SEE ALSO MUSEUMS AND GALLERIES, P.80

The Doge's Palace
See p.93
The Secret Itinerary around the Doge's Palace leads through a maze of murky passageways and alleys, with such added gruesome delights as the torture chamber and prisons, including the stifling *Piombi* or Leads, under the palace eaves.
SEE ALSO PALAZZI, P.93–4

Telecom Italia
Future Centre
Campo di San Salvador; Mon–Fri 9am–noon, 4–7pm; free; vaporetto: Rialto; map p.137 E4
The 16th-century cloisters of the Church of San Salvador is the unlikely setting for a high-tech museum. There are 100 computers that children (and others) can use to access information on the heritage of Venice.

Left: when all else fails, an ice cream usually does the trick.

Try to time your visit to coincide with one of the many festivals celebrated throughout the year, usually accompanied by spectacular firework displays.

Ice cream

By common consent, **Nico's Gelateria** is the best place in Venice for ice cream (Zattere 922, Dorsoduro; closed Thur). The speciality is *gianduiotto*, a blend of hazelnuts, chocolate and whipped cream.

The Lido

It's a good idea for families to book a hotel on the Lido, as many have swimming pools or private beaches – otherwise nearly all the beaches are privately run and only a very few of the luxury hotels in Venice have their own pools. The Lido also offers plenty in the way of cycling, riding, sailing and tennis for older children.
SEE ALSO THE LIDO, P.26–7

Below: traffic-free streets and squares are a communal playground for Venetian children.

In case of a medical emergency, take children to the nearest hospital with an A&E department. In central Venice this is the **Ospedale Civile** in Campo Santi Giovanni e Paolo, tel: 041-529 4111; map p.139 C4.

Scuola di San Giorgio degli Schiavoni
See p.119
Not, perhaps, the obvious choice for children, and not the kind of school they are used to, but San Giorgio is often a surprise hit with younger ones because Carpaccio's paintings are peopled with dragons, knights, princesses and lions.
SEE ALSO SCUOLE, P.119

The Islands

In fine weather take a ferry trip to the islands. **Murano** is famous for glass-making and although children may not be interested in the finished product they will enjoy watching the glass-blowing

Left: *Saint Hieronymus Brings a Lion into the Monastery,* by Carpaccio.

at the workshops along Fondamenta dei Vetrai. Colourful **Burano**, home of fishermen and lace-sellers, is the liveliest of the islands and usually popular with young ones.
SEE ALSO MURANO AND BURANO, P.24–5

Boat Trips

Few can resist a **gondola ride**. A trip on one of these fairy-tale vessels, complete with costumed gondoliers, along the wide sweep of the Grand Canal or through narrow, shady waterways, will be a highlight. Most families can't afford more than one such trip, but a great alternative is offered by the *vaporetti* (waterbuses) or the cheap *traghetti* (gondola ferries) which cross the Grand Canal.

Venice's **waterbuses** will take you up and down the Grand Canal, from end to end, crunching and grinding dramatically as they pull into each stop along the way. If you have very small children there is the added advantage that children under a metre tall can travel free.
SEE ALSO TRANSPORT, P.129–31

Churches

Venice is famous for the number and the beauty of its sacred buildings, from its Byzantine basilicas and majestic monasteries to its sublime Venetian-Gothic and Palladian churches. There seems to be one on every corner. The writer Jan Morris, who knows the city well, wrote 'there are 107 churches in Venice, and nearly every tourist feels he has seen at least 200 of them'. No one would try to see them all, but some are so architecturally beautiful, contain such stunning works of art, or have such a fascinating history, that they should not be missed.

Piazza San Marco

Basilica di San Marco

May–Sep: Mon–Sat 9.45am–5.30pm, Sun 2–4pm, Oct–Apr: Mon–Sat 9.45am–4.30pm, Sun 2–4pm; entrance charge for Pala d'Oro, museum and treasury; vaporetto: San Marco-Vallaresso; map p.138 B2

Consecrated in AD 832, the Basilica was intended as a mausoleum for St Mark's relics and as the doge's ceremonial chapel. It was modelled on Byzantine churches in Constantinople, and designed in the Greek-cross style, crowned by five domes, which are linked to one another by loggias and arcades. The bewildering contrast (art critic John Ruskin called it 'a treasure heap of confusion and delight') is between the oriental domes and rounded Byzantine arches, and the Gothic ornamentation of the central roof line. Gothic arches and pinnacles were grafted onto 12th-century façades and completed by a gallery overlooking the square. Most of the rather garish mosaics on the façade are 17th-century copies of originals, but the interior is studded with glorious mosaics, rich in symbolism. Some of these date from the late 11th century, but mosaics continued to be added until the 18th century. Behind the altar, often swamped by crowds, is the Pala d'Oro, a superb medieval altarpiece, studded with gems and covered in sacred scenes. The panels are enclosed in a gilded frame and encrusted with emeralds, rubies, sapphires and gleaming, translucent enamels bound by gold filigree.

Above: detail of the Pala d'Oro, in the Basilica San Marco, one of the most remarkable works ever produced by medieval goldsmiths.

Sestiere San Marco

San Moisè

Campo San Moisè; Mon–Sat 9.30am–noon; free; vaporetto: San Marco-Vallaresso; map p.138 B1

One of the least-loved churches in Venice, the overlooked San Moisè has a florid Baroque façade. The novelist L.P. Hartley was one of the few to admire its exuberant architecture, with its 'swags, cornucopias and swing boat forms whose lateral movement seemed to rock the church from side to side'.

Left: the glittering façade of the Basilica di San Marco.

whole. The church was founded in the 9th century, and acted as a Venetian pantheon, with eight early doges buried in the crypt. The original Byzantine basilica forms the crypt below San Tarasio chapel, an atmospheric spot usually lying underwater. The chapel itself is decorated with Gothic frescoes and three lovely 15th-century altarpieces. In the north aisle of the main church, which is essentially Gothic, is Bellini's glowing altarpiece, *Madonna and Child*.

San Giorgio dei Greci
Rio dei Greci; Mon–Sat 9.30am–1pm, 3.30–5.30pm, Sun 9am–1pm; free; vaporetto: San Zaccaria; map p.139 D2
The Greek Orthodox church represents one of the oldest ethnic communities in Venice. The 16th-century church has a tall, narrow façade and early-Renaissance purity. In keeping with Orthodox tradition, the interior has a *barco* or *matroneo* (a women's gallery), and an iconostasis, an exotic 16th-century screen separating the sanctuary from

When visiting churches remember to respect the privacy of those who are there to pray; and don't upset local sensibilities by wearing clothes that are too revealing.

Santa Maria Zobenigo (Santa Maria del Giglio)
Rio di Santa Maria Zobenigo (just south of La Fenice); Mon–Sat 10am–5pm; entrance charge; vaporetto: Santa Maria del Giglio; map p.138 A1
A church linked to Antonio Barbaro, a patron who rebuilt it in Baroque style. The façade glorifies the Barbaro dynasty rather than God, with reliefs depicting the dominions governed by the family in the name of the Republic.

Santo Stefano
Campo Santo Stefano; Mon–Sat 10am–5pm, Sun 1–5pm; entrance charge; vaporetto: Accademia; map p.137 D2
This Augustinian monastic church has a Gothic main portal facing a café-lined alley. Unusually, a canal flows under the church, through which gondolas can pass if the tide is low. The interior

has an entrancing ship's-keel ceiling, carved tie beams and, in the rather dark sacristy, notable paintings by Vivarini, Tintoretto and other masters. The tomb of Doge Francesco Morosini (1694) is also prominently displayed in the nave. The cloisters, now appropriated by public offices, are accessible through a gateway in Campo Sant'Angelo.

San Salvador
Campo di San Salvador; Mon–Fri 9am–noon, 4–7pm; free; vaporetto: Rialto; map p.137 E4
Not far from the Rialto stands this luminous Renaissance church, adorned by Titian's impressionistic *Annunciation* and *Transfiguration*.

Castello

San Zaccaria
Campo San Zaccaria; Mon–Sat 10am–noon, 4–6pm; entrance charge to crypt; vaporetto: San Zaccaria; map p.139 C2
This Renaissance masterpiece conceals a far older basilica, with Byzantine and Gothic churches fused into a harmonious Renaissance

Below: Baptistery font, Basilica San Marco.

Basilica di San Marco (St Mark's)

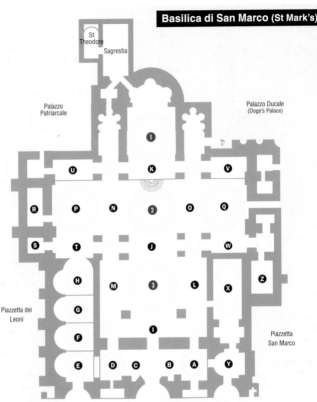

St Theodore

Sagrestia

Palazzo Patriarcale

Palazzo Ducale (Doge's Palace)

Piazzetta dei Leoni

Piazzetta San Marco

Piazza San Marco

Sights of Interest

A Creation and the Fall of Man

B Story of Noah and the Flood

C Tower of Babel

D Story of Abraham

E Story of Joseph

F Joseph is Sold to Potiphar

G Joseph Rules Egypt

H Story of Moses

I Saviour between the Virgin and St Mark, Scenes from the Apocalypse, Last Judgement

J The Passion, the Kiss of Judas until the Crucifixion

K Scenes from the Life of Christ

L The Passion, the Agony in the Garden

M Christ and the Apostles

N Christ Pantocrator

O Scenes from the Life of Christ

P Deeds of John the Evangelist

Q St Nicola, St Clemente, St Biagio, St Leonardo

R Cappella di Sant'Isidoro

S Cappella della Madonna dei Mascoli

T Mosaics illustrating the Life of the Virgin

U Cappella della Madonna Nicopeia

V Altare del Sacramento

W Madonna del Bacio, Madonna of the Kiss

X Battistero (Baptistery)

Y Cappella Zen (Zeno chapel)

Z Tesoro (Treasury)

The Domes

1 Dome of the Altar

2 Dome of the Ascension

3 Dome of the Pentecost

Above: the Baroque campanile of Santa Maria Formosa.

the nave. This intimate church comes alive during the vibrant Easter festivals, when the stylised, golden interior and the scent of incense create a heady exoticism.

Santa Maria Formosa
Campo Santa Maria Formosa; Mon–Sat 10am–5pm, Sun 1–5pm; entrance charge; vaporetto: San Zaccaria or Rialto; map p.138 C3

This parish church is an endearing sight, with its eccentrically bulging apses. The foundations may date from the 9th century, but the church was redesigned by Coducci, the great Renaissance architect, and later acquired a Baroque belltower with a grotesque mask at its base. The campo façade was added in 1604. The cool grey-and-white marble interior contains two Venetian masterpieces: Bartolomeo Vivarini's triptych of *The Madonna of the Misericordia* (1473) and Palma il Vecchio's polyptych of *St Barbara and Saints* (c.1522).

Santi Giovanni e Paolo
Campo Santi Giovanni e Paolo; Mon–Sat 7.30am–12.30pm, 3–6.30pm, Sun 3–7pm; entrance charge; vaporetto: Ospedale; map p.139 C4

Familiarly known as San Zanipolo, this huge brick edifice vies with the Frari as the largest Gothic church in Venice. Known as the Pantheon of Venice, it is full of tombs and monuments to doges and other dignataries. In the chancel lies the finest Renaissance funerary monument in Venice, dedicated to Doge Andrea Vendramin who died in 1478. The Chapel of the Rosary has ceiling panels by Veronese, considered the most pagan and joyous of Venetian painters. The church interior is enriched by other lovely works of art, including Vivarini's *Christ Bearing the Cross* (1474). In the right aisle, Bellini's gorgeous St Vincent Ferrier altarpiece is set in its original gilded frame.

San Francesco della Vigna
Rio di San Francesco; daily 8am–noon, 3.30–7pm; free; vaporetto: Celestia map p.139 D3

The name 'della Vigna' derives from the vineyard that was here before the land was given to the Franciscans. The church was Sansovino's first creation; the façade and crowning pediment were added later by Palladio, and the tall bell tower is a familiar city landmark. Highlights include sculptures from the Lombardi school, Veronese's *Holy Family with Saints*, and a *Madonna and Child* by Negroponte (1450). The lovely Gothic cloisters lead to the Cappella Santa where a Giovanni Bellini *Madonna* can be found.

San Giovanni in Bragora
Campo San Giovanni in Bragora; Mon–Sat 9–11am, 3.30–5.30pm; free; vaporetto: Arsenale; map p.139 D2

This austere church is essentially late-Gothic, despite 9th-century foundations and a Renaissance presbytery. The interior is notable for its Renaissance works of art. While Bartolomeo Vivarini's *Madonna and Saints* (1478) is a stiff, Byzantine-style work, his nephew Alvise shows humanist leanings in his *Resurrection* (1498), a dynamic altarpiece. Adorning the high altar is Cima da Conegliano's *Baptism of Christ* (1492-5), set against a realistic mountain landscape. Vivaldi was baptised in the red marble font, as the proudly-displayed copies of the baptismal register prove.

La Pietà
Riva degli Schiavoni; daily 10am–noon, 4–6pm; free; vaporetto: San Zaccaria; 139 D2

The Pietà (or Santa Maria della Visitazione) is known as 'Vivaldi's church' as he directed music groups here and wrote pieces for the Pietà choir. The Ospedale della Pietà was the most famous of the *ospedali* – institutions that combined the roles of orphanage and musical conservatoire. Such was its popularity that parents tried to

Below: Santi Giovanni e Paolo, the Pantheon of Venice.

pass off their children as orphans. A plaque which you can still see on the side of the church threatens damnation to anyone who attempted to do so. The gleaming gold-and-white church interior is crowned by Tiepolo's *Triumph of Faith* (1755). In the dazzling fresco, the figures appear to come alive and billow into the church itself.

San Pietro di Castello
Campo di San Pietro; Mon–Sat 10am–5pm, Sun 1–5pm; entrance charge; vaporetto: Giardini; map p.140 B3

Built on ancient foundations, this is a Palladian structure with a central dome. The church was the city's Cathedral from 1451 until 1807, while San Marco was merely the doge's private chapel.

Cannaregio

Gesuiti
Campo dei Gesuiti; daily 10am–noon, 4–6pm; free; vaporetto: Fondamenta Nuove; map p.137 C1

The design of the Gesuiti is typical of a Roman Jesuit church, with a broad nave flanked by deep chapels and surmounted by a central

dome. The impression is of a wedding cake swathed in green-and-white damask, even if it is marble masquerading as drapery. The highlights are Titian's stormy *Martyrdom of St Lawrence* and Tintoretto's joyous *Assumption of the Virgin*, the painting that most inspired Tiepolo.

Oratorio dei Crociferi
Campo dei Gesuiti; Fri–Sat 3.30–6.30pm; entrance charge; vaporetto: Fondamenta Nuove; map p.135 E2

Facing the Gesuiti, this church is dedicated to the crusading mendicant Order of Crutched Friars, but later passed into Jesuit control. The interior has a subtle pictorial cycle by Palma il Giovane (1548–1628).

Santi Apostoli
Campo Santi Apostoli; daily 8–11.30am, 5–7pm; free; vaporetto: Ca' d'Oro; map p.135 E1

The 16th-century church is built on ancient foundations but is undistinguished, apart from Tiepolo's *Communion of St Lucy*, set in the domed Renaissance Corner Chapel.

Santa Maria dei Miracoli
Campo dei Miracoli; Mon–Sat 10am–5pm, Sun 1–5pm;

Above: San Sebastiano, Dorsoduro *(see p.44).*

entrance charge; vaporetto: Rialto; map p.135 E1

The romantic waterside setting of this lovely church invites such clichés as 'Renaissance jewel box', and makes it a favourite with Venetian brides. Inside, the surfaces present a vision of pale pinks and silvery greys, the pilasters adorned with interlaced flowers, mythical creatures and cavorting mermaids.

Madonna dell'Orto
Campo della Madonna dell'Orto; Mon–Sat 10am–5pm, Sun 1–5pm; entrance charge; vaporetto: Madonna dell'Orto; map p.135 D4

This masterpiece of the Venetian Gothic is conspicuous for its campanile with the onion-shaped cupola, the richly embellished brick façade and beautiful carved portal. It was named after a miracle-working statue of the Madonna found in a nearby vegetable garden (*orto*), and is now displayed in the Mauro Chapel. This was Tintoretto's parish church, and the artist is buried in the chapel to the right of the altar. The austere, brick-faced interior, graced by Greek marble columns and a fine wooden ceiling, was finely

Below: interior of Santa Maria dei Miracoli, a Renaissance gem in Cannaregio *(see p.42).*

restored by the British Venice in Peril fund after the 1966 floods. The church showcases Tintoretto paintings, including *Presentation of the Virgin* (1551) and two works dominating the chancel: *The Last Judgement* and *The Adoration of the Golden Calf*. Tintoretto aside, the church is a treasury of Venetian painting from the 15th–17th centuries.

San Giovanni Crisostomo

Campo Giovanni Crisostomo; daily 8.30am–noon, 3.30–7pm; vaporetto: Rialto; map p.135 E1

Crammed into a little square north of the Rialto this Renaissance church was Mauro Coducci's last work. The restrained marble interior contains a delightful Bellini altarpiece (1515), possibly his last work, executed when he was in his 80s. The dome, supported by pillars and arches, is a model of Classical coherence.

San Polo

I Frari

Campo dei Frari; Mon–Sat 9am–6pm, Sun 1–6pm; entrance charge; vaporetto: San Tomà; map p.137 C4

The great bulk of the Frari, founded in the 13th century, is virtually devoid of ornamentation, in keeping with the principles of the Franciscan order. The high altar is the focal point of the Frari, a space illuminated by Titian's *Assumption*, flanked by dogal tombs. His other great work, the Pesaro Altarpiece, lies in the north aisle of the nave. There are altarpieces by Vivarini and Bellini and the choir chapels are lined with tombs of the doges. Titian's bombastic tomb is also here, as is the mausoleum of Canova.

San Giacomo di Rialto

Ruga degli Orefici; Mon–Sat 10am–5pm, Sun 1–5pm; free; vaporetto: Rialto; map p.138 B3

Affectionately known as San Giacometto, this is the oldest church in Venice, founded in the 5th century, rebuilt in the 11th. Its most distinctive features are the Gothic portico, belltower and bold 24-hour clock. The 16th-century restoration respected the original domed Greek-cross plan, Greek columns and Veneto-Byzantine capitals.

San Polo

Campo San Polo; Mon–Sat 10am–5pm, Sun 1-5pm; entrance charge; vaporetto: San Tomà; map p.137 D4

Essentially Gothic, the church features a rose window, ship's-keel ceiling and some notable paintings, including a *Last Supper* by Tintoretto and Giandomenico Tiepolo's *Via Crucis* – 14 canvases of the Stations of the Cross.

Santa Croce

San Giacomo dell'Orio

Campo San Giacomo dell'Orio; Mon–Sat 10am–5pm, Sun 1–5pm; entrance charge; vaporetto: Riva di Biasio or San Stae; map p.134 C1

The church spans many centuries since its 9th century foundation. Behind the pulpit and in the right transept are several Byzantine capitals raided from Constantinople, including one made of greenish Greek marble. The pièce de résistance is the Gothic ship's-keel roof. The finest artworks are a rare 14th-century wooden Tuscan crucifix and, in the New Sacristy, a Veronese ceiling.

Below: I Frari, officially known as Santa Maria Gloriosa dei Frari. The hulking Franciscan complex is the largest of all the Venetian Gothic churches.

> Henry James said La Salute was 'like some great lady on the threshold of her salon. She is ample and serene… with her domes and scrolls… forming a pompous crown.'

San Simeone Piccolo
Fondamenta di San Simeone Piccolo; Mon–Sat 10am–5pm; free; vaporetto: Ferrovia or Piazzale Roma; map p.134 B1

This church was modelled on the Pantheon in Rome and created as a counter-weight to La Salute *(see below)*, framing the Grand Canal with a Baroque church at either end.

Dorsoduro

Gesuati
Zattere; Mon–Sat 10am–5pm, Sun 1–5pm; entrance charge; vaporetto: Zattere; map p.135 E2

Commissioned by the Dominicans, the church dates from 1726. Tiepolo masterpieces adorn the vaulted ceiling, his Madonna altarpiece graces one of the chapels, and there is also a sombre Tintoretto Crucifixion.

La Salute
Campo della Salute; daily 9am–5.30pm; entrance charge to Sacristy; vaporetto: Salute; map p.137 E1

This grandiose basilica was begun in 1630, but took 50 years to complete. Designed by Longhena, it mingles the Classical with the Baroque. Devised before Rome's Bernini and Borromini masterpieces, it became one of the few Italian churches to challenge the supremacy of Roman Baroque. The interior has a spectacular central plan, with its revolutionary octagonal space surmounted by a huge dome. The major works of art are in the Sacristy and include works by Tintoretto and Titian and a

Above: the open timber roof of Santa Maria Assunta, Burano.

small Byzantine Madonna, overawed by Baroque splen-dour. At a November festival, gondoliers brings their oars here to be blessed.

San Pantalon
Campo San Pantalon; Mon–Sat 8–10am, 4–6pm; free; vaporetto: San Tomà; map p.136 C3

A bare, 17th-century façade conceals a highly theatrical interior. The Baroque ceiling-paintings by Fumiani (1650–1710) depict *The Martyrdom and Glory of St Pantalon*. This was created on 60 panels and hoisted into place. The illusionistic ascent into heaven is populated by boldly fore-shortened figures clambering, floating or ascending. Veronese's last work, *The Miracle of St Pantalon*, is in a chapel on the right.

San Nicolò dei Mendicoli
Campo San Nicolò; Mon–Sat 10am–noon, 4–6pm; free; vaporetto: San Basilio ; map p.136 A2

Founded in the 7th century and later remodelled, this is one of the oldest churches in Venice, and one of the best loved. Distinctive aspects

include the Byzantine cor-nices and a nave graced by Romanesque columns, Gothic capitals and beamed ceilings. A single nave ends in a Romanesque apse; and the walls are embellished with Renaissance panelling and school of Veronese paintings.

San Sebastiano
Rio di San Sebastiano; Mon–Sat 10am–5pm, Sun 1–5pm; entrance charge; vaporetto: San Basilio; map p.136 A2

This 16th-century church is a showcase for many of Veronese's masterpieces, showing him in all his glory, exalting grace, harmony and serenity while indulging in occasional whimsy. His trompe l'oeil interior is an architectural flight of fancy created by frescoed loggias, columns and statues. Blocks of pure colour adorn every surface, from the nave ceiling to the organ panels. The indi-vidual subjects are secondary to the overall effect, a broad spectrum of religious, histori-cal and mythological motifs.

Santa Maria dei Carmini
Campo dei Carmini; Mon–Sat 2.30–5pm; free; vaporetto: Ca' Rezzonico; map p.136 B2

Below: San Giorgio Maggiore, a Palladian masterpiece.

> Outside Santa Maria dell' Assunta on Torcello lie the vestiges of a 7th-century baptistery, built on a circular plan like the Roman baths; and Attila's Throne, a Roman potentate's marble seat.

The solemn nave has 17th-century arcades and a number of ponderous Baroque paintings. The finest Renaissance painting is Cima da Conegliano's *Nativity* in the second altar on the right.

Giudecca and San Giorgio Maggiore Islands

Il Redentore
Campo Redentore, Giudecca; Mon–Sat 10am–5pm, Sun 1–5pm; entrance charge; vaporetto: Redentore; map p.22
This Palladian masterpiece has a recently restored façade, floodlit at night, with a sweeping flight of steps echoing the style of a gracious country villa. From here, the eye is led to the lantern surmounted by a figure of Christ the Redeemer. Palladio was influenced by contemporary Roman architecture, and Il Redentore's choir echoes Bramante's plan for St Peter's.

San Giorgio Maggiore
Daily 9.30am–12.30pm, 2.30–6.30pm; vaporetto: San Giorgio Maggiore; map p.22
In 1565 Palladio was commissioned to rebuild the church here, his finest Venetian legacy, rivalled only by Il Redentore. Here Palladio shows his mastery of the Classical idiom, using the basic geometric volumes of cube, pyramid and sphere. The cool church is a model of perspective, with a domed interior which is bathed in white light. Although most visitors

restrict their visit to the church and bell tower (there's a lift to the top), to appreciate the size and diversity of the monastic site, you need to tour the Cini Foundation *(see p.82)*.

Murano and Burano

Santi Maria e Donato
Fondamenta Giustinian; 8.30am–noon, 3.30–7pm; free; vaporetto: Museo; map p.24
This is the finest church on Murano, a 7th-century structure remodelled in Veneto-Byzantine style. The brick and terracotta 12th-century apses are studded with zigzag friezes and dog-tooth mouldings. The apse is dominated by a luminous Byzantine-style mosaic of the Madonna and Child, rivalled by a beautiful altarpiece by Paolo Veneziano (c.1310). The highlight is the patterned mosaic floor, depicting interlaced foliage and allegorical animals.

Torcello

Santa Fosca
Daily 10.30am–6pm; free; vaporetto: Torcello
Built by Greeks in the 11th century, Santa Fosca was

designed to house the relics of a martyr. The church is a coherent masterpiece, a harmonious structure combining Romanesque with Byzantine elements.

Santa Maria dell'Assunta
Daily 10.30am–6pm; combined ticket with museum and bell-tower; vaporetto: Torcello
Linked by a portico to Santa Fosca, this is a model of an early Christian church. It is the oldest monument in the lagoon, founded in AD 639 as an episcopal seat. The basilica was modelled on those in Ravenna, but modified in the 9th and early 11th centuries to create a superb Veneto-Byzantine building. The dignified interior is punctuated by slender Greek marble columns, bearing Byzantine capitals. The church was first restored in 1008, with the raising of the floor and creation of a crypt: the lovely mosaic floor dates from this period. Among the treasures are the original 7th-century altar, the pulpit, the ceremonial throne and a Roman sarcophagus.

The recently restored bell tower has some fine views of the lagoon.

Below: The basilica of Santi Maria e Donato, Murano.

45

Environment

Venice has always been threatened by winter floods, but it was the massive flood of 1966 that mobilised the world, provoking a debate about restoration that's still ongoing. Although the city officially stopped sinking in 1983, subsidence, partly caused by the sheer weight of the buildings is still a problem, as are the threats of further flooding and tidal erosion. Venice's unique situation means that the city has many would-be saviours, from Venice in Peril, Save Venice and Unesco, to the Green lobby and the Italian government. Venice's problems are many, but aquatic extinction is still some way off.

Acqua Alta

Acqua alta (high water) is one of the city's biggest problems, and occurs when south-easterly sirocco winds combine with tides to trap the high water in the lagoon. Currently cranes punctuate the quayside at San Marco, and other vulnerable waterfronts, as the levels are raised to prevent further flooding. Global warming, human intervention and industrialisation are all to blame for the *acqua alta*. The 20th century saw the delicate balance of the lagoon disturbed by land reclamation, the deepening of shipping channels and the enclosure of sections for fish farming.

Sinking no More

Venice officially stopped sinking in 1983, after the extraction of underground water was forbidden. The drawing of millions of gallons of water from artesian wells in Porto Marghera (the industrial centre on the mainland) had led to a sharp fall in the water table and threatened subsidence. In the 1970s

Above: environmental demonstrators on the lagoon.

aqueducts were built to pipe water from inland rivers to the industrial zone. But Venetian subsidence is partly caused by the weight of the city, with many monuments under threat. Buildings are supported by wooden piles driven deep into the mudflats; change in the water levels means that at low tides the piles are exposed to the air, causing decay.

Venice in Peril

In the wake of the 1966 floods, under the umbrella of Unesco, some 30 private organisations from around the world, including the US's Save Venice Foundation, went into action to save the city. Britain's Venice in Peril has been a major contributor to the restoration of monuments (see www.venice inperil.org).

The Moses Project

Named *Mose* (Moses) after the biblical figure who parted the waves, a new tidal barrier, scheduled for completion in 2011, is set to save Venice from perilous floods. Ex-Prime Minister Silvio Berlusconi laid the foundation stone for the long-awaited project in 2003, but work since then has been frequently obstructed by protests from environmental campaigners. The barrier is being installed across the three lagoon inlets, using steel floodgates lying on the seabed to form a submerged barrage. If dangerous tides threaten, air is pumped into the gates and the barrier springs into action. The authorities have also

Left: a gondolier gives way
to a garbage barge.

The wash from the *vaporetti* on
the canals causes erosion,
eating away at the stonework
of Grand Canal palaces, and
has led to the closure of certain
ferry routes. *Vaporetti* ticket
prices for tourists have all been
hiked up to restrict the number
of travellers and minimise
further decay.

strengthened the coastal
defences and reinstated
sandbanks. The lagoon's 60-
km outer coastline has been
reinforced with artificial reefs
and new beaches backed by
breakwaters. Yet many environmentalists are against
Mose, which will only operate in cases of severe flooding; the regular flooding of
the low-lying San Marco area
will still occur. Instead, they
favour letting the tides regu-
late themselves, halting land-
reclamation, letting shipping
lanes revert to their original
paths, and creating a cruise
terminal outside the lagoon.

Pollution

Over the years, the Mestre-
Marghera industrial complex
on the mainland has
dumped tons of pollutants
into the lagoon. The pro-
posed solution is to lay
pipelines to take the waste
out to sea. Toxic fumes from
the port are also damaging
Venice's fragile buildings and
statuary. Venice itself is not
blameless. While domestic
sewage is treated, baths and
sinks still drain into the
canals. Phosphate-enriched
household detergents have
been banned as plant and
marine life in the lagoon
were suffocated by the algae
that thrive on them. Venice is
finally taking its responsibili-
ties seriously, and has
embarked on a programme
to consolidate the city foundations, both in Venice and
on the islands of Giudecca
and the Lido, and salt
marshes and wetlands are
being reinstated on the edge
of the lagoon.

Population Decline

Ordinary people cannot
afford to live in Venice and
the population has halved
since 1945. As the cost of
housing and restoration
rises, Venetians have been
leaving the city for cheaper
accommodation on the
mainland. The population of
the historic centre has fallen
to 61,000, with a further
45,000 living on the outlying
islands and 190,000 on the
mainland. More than 30,000
people commute into the
city, mostly to work in a
tourist industry that serves
more than 15 million visitors
a year.

Below: an empty Caffè Quadri reflected in flood waters on
St Mark's Square.

Essentials

Although Venice is unique in being a city built on water, visitors will find that in many other ways it shares characteristics with other European cities; from the currency to the electrical voltage. It is also a city that has had a tourist industry for a very long time and is therefore used to dealing with tourists smoothly and efficiently. The information given below is designed to serve as a useful check-list for basic information and emergency procedures. Further practical information on hotels, transport and shopping is provided in the separate dedicated sections.

Electricity

The standard is 220 volts. You will need an adaptor to operate UK three-pin appliances and a transformer for US 100 to 120-volt appliances.

Emergencies

For **police**, tel: 112/113; **ambulance**, tel: 118; **fiire brigade**, tel: 115; **Venice city police**, tel: 041-274 7070; **British consulate**, Piazzale Donatori di Sangue, 2, Mestre (on the mainland), tel: 041-505 5990. Nearest **US consulate**: Largo Donegani 1, Milan, tel: 02-290 351.

Health

Before travelling, ensure you have a valid health insurance policy. Citizens of the UK and other EU countries are entitled to free reciprocal health care (from participating doctors/hospitals) if they have a European Health Insurance Card (in the UK, check

Metric to Imperial Conversions
Metres–Feet 1=3.28
Kilometres–Miles 1=0.62
Hectares–Acres 1=2.47
Kilograms–Pounds 1=2.2

www.ehic.org.uk. If you are seriously ill, telephone 118 or go to the *Pronto Soccorso* (casualty department) of the nearest hospital. In central Venice, this is the **Ospedale Civile**, Campo Santi Giovanni e Paolo (San Zanipolo), tel: 041-529 4111, also accessible by water taxi. On the Lido, tel: 041-526 1750.

Italian pharmacists are qualified to advise on minor health complaints. Night pharmacists (*farmacie*) operate on a rota system; consult your hotel or check the sign posted on any pharmacist's window.

Tap-water is generally safe to drink, but Venetians prefer mineral water. Take mosquito repellent with you, especially in the hot summer months.

Money

The unit of currency is the euro. Banknotes are available in denominations of 5, 10, 20, 50, 100, 200 and 500 euros; there are coins for 1, 2, 5, 10, 20 and 50 cents, and 1 and 2 euros. Banks open Monday–Friday 8.30am–1.30pm and usually also from 2.30–3.30pm. You will need your

Above: the 'Poste Italiane' is not known for its speed.

passport when changing money. ATMs are plentiful and have instructions in English and other languages. Most hotels do not accept travellers' cheques. Major credit cards are accepted by most good stores and restaurants, but are less common than in the US or Northern Europe. Banks, which give a more favourable rate of exchange than foreign-exchange offices, are plentiful around

Left: news stand near Piazzale Roma.

Under 29s are entitled to the excellent value RollingVenice card, which gives discounts on accommodation, restaurants, museums, shops and public transport. The pass costs three euros and is available from tourist offices on presentation of ID and a passport photo.

The **Hello Venezia Call Centre** (www.hellovenezia.it; tel: 041-2424) is open daily 7.30am–8pm for information on public transport, museums, theatres and sporting events. The tourist discount Venicecard can be bought here, and guided tours of La Fenice and some cultural events can be booked via the centre.

the San Marco and Rialto areas of the city.

Post

Post offices generally open Monday–Friday 8.30am–2pm, Saturday 8.30am–1pm. The main post office is at the Fondaco dei Tedeschi on the St Mark's side of the Rialto (8.30am–6.30pm).

Stamps (*francobolli*) are also available from tobacconists (*tabacchi*) displaying a white 'T' and some card shops. If you need to send an urgent letter, ask for *posta prioritaria*.

Telephones

There are lots of public telephones, though most only accept phone cards (*schede telefoniche*) and coins. The cards are sold at news-stands and *tabacchi* (tobacconists) and come in denominations of €2.50, €5 and €10. At the main Telecom Italia office in Piazzale Roma (8am–9.30pm) and the main post office *(see above)* you can dial direct and pay upon completion of the call. If calling from a hotel, expect a steep mark-up. You can also purchase prepaid international phone cards (from €5) which are excellent value for calling abroad. For these you need to dial a toll-free number found on the back of the card.

To call Venice from abroad, dial +39-041 plus the number. If calling Venice from within Italy, including from within Venice itself, dial 041, plus the number.

Tourist Offices

St Mark's

APT at the Venice Pavilion, Giardini Ex Reali, beside Piazza San Marco; tel: 041-522 5150; daily 10am-6pm.

The office has a good bookshop and sells tickets for concerts and other events.

Calle dell'Ascensione/Procuratie Nuove

tel: 041-529 8711, daily 9am–3.30pm

A smaller, busier office. on the western corner of Piazza San Marco opposite the entrance of the Correr Museum.

Santa Lucia railway station

Daily 8am–6.30pm

Marco Polo airport

9.30am–7.30pm

This mostly deals with accommodation and transport tickets.

The official tourist board website is www.turismovenezia.it. Another useful site is www.comune.venezia.it

Below: public phone boxes are still widely used.

Festivals

V enice is known for its carnival, an exuberant, over-the-top celebration held each February or March, and for the Biennale, a high-profile celebration of contemporary art and architecture staged every other year. Both events draw crowds from around the world. But there are numerous other festivals to celebrate throughout the year, from the famous International Film Festival, to colourful water festivals and regattas commemorating saints' days or historic events, usually accompanied by spectacular firework displays. Chances are there will be some celebration you can join during your stay.

Carnival

The Venetian Carnival, a pre-Lent celebration whose date depends on that of Easter, took place throughout the years of the Republic. It disappeared after Napoleon conquered Venice in 1797 and was restored in the 20th century. A 10-day extravaganza of masked balls, street revelry, concerts and pantomime, the high point comes on Shrove Tuesday with a masked ball in Piazza San Marco, after which the effigy of Carnival is burned in the square.

Festa di San Marco

Honouring the city's patron saint, this festival on April 25 is marked by a gondola race from the island of Sant'Elena to the Punta della Dogana at the entrance of the Grand Canal, and the consumption of *risi e bisi*, a thick rice-and-pea soup.

Festa della Sensa

Held in May on the Sunday after Ascension Day, this is a re-enactment of the Marriage of Venice with the Sea fol-

Above: fireworks blazing over the lagoon.

lowed by a regatta off the Lido. Until the fall of the Republic, the doge would sail from San Marco to the Lido in the *Bucintoro*, the state barge, and ceremonially cast a ring into the water.

Vogalonga

On the Sunday following La Sensa (see above) the Voga-longa ('long row') involves hundreds of rowing boats following a course from San Marco to Burano and back: about 32km. This is a free-for-all and anyone with an oar-powered craft can take part.

Art Biennale

Held from June to November in alternate (odd) years, this grand contemporary art show is staged in the Giardini Pubblici (Public Gardens), the Corderie, the old rope factory in the Arsenale, and other city locations (www.labiennale.org). In even numbered years, the Architecture Biennale is held in the Giardini pavilions.

La Festa del Redentore

The Feast of the Redeemer, in July, is the most touching and intimate of Venetian festivals. It focuses on Il Redentore, the church built as a token of thanks for salvation from the plague of 1575–57. Venetians wend their way to the church, carrying candles and reciting the rosary. A sweeping bridge of boats stretches across the Giudecca canal to the

Left: Venice's kitsch masquerade retains its magic.

Burano also includes a lively music festival.

Festival Galuppi

Another September festival, this one named after a Burano composer, stages concerts on the island and also in a number of venues in central Venice, including La Salute.

La Festa della Madonna della Salute

Celebrated on 21 November, this is another festival commemorating the city's deliverance from a devastating plague, this one in 1630, with recorded casualties of around 46,000 out of a population of 140,000. There is a votive procession to the church, reached by a pontoon bridge from Santa Maria del Giglio. Venetians make the pilgrimage to La Salute to light candles in gratitude for the continuing good health of the city and its citizens. This Baroque church makes a spectacular sight, its main doors flung open and crowds ascending the steps.

> If you are coming to Venice for Carnival or any of the major festivals be sure to book flights and accommodation well in advance – and be prepared for higher prices.

church. The spectacular firework display on the eve of the feast day has been a feature since the 16th century. At night, crowds line the Zattere and the Giudecca or take to boats of every description, which are bedecked in finery and glow with lights.

Film Festival

A 10-day event in September on the Lido. It is art-house films that tend to win the awards but the festival attracts a glitzy Hollywood crowd. Events become extremely cosmopolitan, centred on the Lido by day, and San Marco by night.

La Regata Storica

The Historic Regatta, on the first Sunday in September, is the finest regatta in Venice. It dates from 1825, and was a way of preserving the great memories of the Republic. The cavalcade of boats winds its way from the Giardini quarter to Ca' Foscari on the Grand Canal, where prizes are presented from dignitaries gathered on a decorated barge. It is followed by a gondola race.

Sagra del Pesce

The September fish festival and regatta on the island of

Below: the glamorous summer forum for contemporary art is held in odd-numbered years.

Film

Venice is the home of the world's oldest film festival, founded by Mussolini in 1932. For 10 days in late August/early September the city plays host to a huge cast of Hollywood and European stars, and the attendant paparazzi. The presentation of the Leone d'Oro award in the newly restored La Fenice opera house is a glittering occasion. Venice does not have a film industry, but it has been the backdrop – if not the star – of a number of well-known films. Recently the festival has gone all out for Hollywood glitz, even if worthy art-house winners tend to triumph in the end.

The Film Festival

The annual Film Festival is centred on the **Palazzo del Cinemà** *(see p.26–7)*, built in the 1930s in triumphant Fascist style. To spot the celebrities stroll along the beachside boulevard or splash out on a cocktail at the sea view terrace of the Hotel Excelsior. Most tickets go to the film and press industries but there are some tickets available to the general public. For information check www.labiennale.org.

Cinemas

Venice has a number of cinemas, key ones include the **Accademia** (in Dorsoduro) and the **Rossini** (opposite the church of San Luca in San Marco). **Giorgione Movie**, at Cannaregio 4612, usually shows foreign films in

Most foreign films shown in Italy are dubbed into Italian. *Versione originale* (original version) or *VO* on posters or in listings indicates that films are presented in their own language.

their original language *(VO)*. (Take vaporetto Line No. 1 to the Ca' d'Oro stop.)

In mid-summer the Campo San Polo makes a splendid setting for open-air cinema, with film shows every evening.

Set in Venice

THE MERCHANT OF VENICE
Al Pacino stars as Shylock and Jeremy Irons as Antonio in Michael Radford's acclaimed 2004 version of Shakespeare's tragic tale, set in 16th-century Venice. The city provides a suitably murky background for scenes in which the reviled Shylock seeks his revenge.

DON'T LOOK NOW
Nicolas Roeg's 1973 film starring Julie Christie and Donald Sutherland lingers in the mind. Based on a short story by Daphne du Maurier, it is the tale of a couple who go to Venice while grieving over the death of their young daughter. Once there, they become embroiled in strange, apparently supernatural, happenings, made more

Above: Dirk Bogarde in Visconti's *Death in Venice*.

chilling by the muted tones of wintry Venice in which they take place.

DEATH IN VENICE
Luchino Visconti's 1971 film is perhaps the one most closely associated with the city. Based on Thomas Mann's 1912 novel, it stars Dirk Bogarde as Gustav von Aschenbach, a composer who falls in

Left: Daniel Craig brandishes his weapon in *Casino Royale*.

and Susan Anspach moves to Venice when Segal's lovesick lawyer character returns to the city where he had spent his honeymoon six years earlier.

VENICE/VENICE

So good they named it twice... The film was not a big hit, however, although the plot – an American film director in Venice to promote his entry in the festival – makes good use of the city and the media circus that erupts at festival time. Made in 1992, it starred the then little known David Duchovny, who went on to star in *The X Files*.

JAMES BOND

The well-travelled Mr Bond showed up in Venice in several of his films. He pops up briefly in *From Russia With Love* (1963), manages to drive a gondola on land in *Moonraker* (1979), and has all kinds of Venetian adventures in the highly acclaimed 2006 version of *Casino Royal*.

love with a Polish boy while staying at the **Hôtel des Bains** on the **Lido**. The translucent light of the Lido makes an atmospheric background for this poignant story.

THE ENGLISH PATIENT

Venice played no part in this story of wartime love and loss but the Belle-Epoque **Hôtel des Bains** on the **Lido** was used as a location for scenes that were supposed to take place in Cairo.

EVERYONE SAYS I LOVE YOU

Directed by Woody Allen in 1996, and starring Allen, Alan Alda, Goldie Hawn, Drew Barrymore and Julia Roberts, this off-the-wall musical comedy featured many scenes set along the **Grand Canal** and in the narrow back streets.

THE TALENTED MR RIPLEY

Anthony Minghella's adaptation of the Patricia Highsmith novel concerning assumed identity – starring Matt Damon, Gwyneth Paltrow, Jude Law and Cate Blanchett – used Venice as a backdrop for its beautiful people.

DANGEROUS BEAUTY

Starring Rufus Sewell and Catherine McCormack, this passionate film depicts the life of courtesan Veronica Franco and captures the atmosphere of 16th-century Venice, when it lorded over the Mediterranean.

BLUME IN LOVE

This 1973 romantic comedy, directed by Paul Mazursky and starring George Segal

Below: the *Leone d'Oro*, or 'Golden Lion' is the prize awarded at the film festival.

53

Food and Drink

Some critics damn Venetian food as over-priced and underachieving, but you can eat very well if you choose wisely. Avoid the grim tourist menus and seek out places slightly off the beaten track and you will be rewarded with good food in pleasant surroundings. For those who love seafood and white wine, the experience can be memorable; and those with a sweet tooth are rarely disappointed. If you are self-catering, or just want a taste of the real Venice, head for the Rialto market.

Culinary Cultures

As the hub of a cosmopolitan trading empire, Venice once bristled with foreign communities – Arabs, Armenians, Greeks, Jews and Turks – each with its own culinary tradition. Venetian trading posts in the Levant gave the city access to spices, which are the secret of subtle Venetian cookery. Pimiento, turmeric, ginger, cinnamon, cumin, cloves, nutmeg, saffron and vanilla show the oriental influences; pinenuts, raisins, almonds and pistac-hios also play their part.

From the end of the 18th century, French influence meant that oriental spices were supplanted by Mediterranean herbs.

Compared with other big cities, most restaurants close early in Venice, around 10.30pm, with last orders often well before 10pm. However some of the new nightspots *(see p.86–9)* serve food until the early hours of the morning.

Seafood

Fish and seafood are Venetian staples. It is hard to better *antipasti di frutti di mare,* a feast of simply-cooked seafood: prawns, soft-shelled crabs, baby octopus and squid. Trademark dishes are cuttlefish risotto, served black and pungent with ink; *granse-ola* (spider crab), boiled and dressed in lemon and oil; or *moleche,* small soft-shelled crabs fried with oil, garlic and

herbs and eaten whole; and *seppie alla veneziana,* cuttle-fish in its own ink, served with polenta. Two other staples are *baccalà,* dried salt cod, pre-pared with milk and herbs or sometimes with parmesan and parsley; and *sarde in saor,* marinated sardines.

Seafood with pasta is popular: try *pappardelle alla granseola* (pasta with crab), *spaghetti con astice* (with lobster), or *bigoli,* black strands of spaghetti served in *salsa* (anchovy or tuna sauce). A variety of seafood dishes use tiny sea snails *(garuzoli),* mussels *(cozze)* and cuttlefish *(seppie).*

Meat Dishes

Although seafood is the Venetian speciality, good

Below: fresh produce at the Rialto market.

Left: a plate of *cichetti*.

best-known white, comes from vineyards along the eastern shores of Lake Garda. Dry whites from the Veneto and Friuli, such as Soave or Pinot Grigio, bring out the best in seafood dishes. As a refreshing aperitif there is little to beat a chilled glass of Prosecco or Cartizzi, sparkling white wines from the Veneto. Another popular sparkling drink is spritz, a combination of dry white wine, soda water and Campari or Aperol.

meat dishes can also be found. One of the best is *fegato alla veneziana* (tender calf's liver sliced into ribbons and cooked with parsley and onion), served with polenta. *Vitello tonnato* (thin slices of cold veal fillet in tuna sauce) is also a good dish to try.

Vegetables

Minestra (soup) such as *pasta e fasioi*, based on pasta and beans is a typical *primo* (first course). *Melanzane in saor* is aubergines in a spicy sauce made with permutations of onions, raisins, vinegar, pine-nuts and olive oil (*saor* means savoury or tasty). *Riso* (rice) has been prized for its versatility ever since its introduction by the Arabs. Creamy Venetian risotto offers endless possibilities, flavoured with spring vegetables, meat, game or fish. *Risi e bisi* (rice and peas) is a thick soup blended with ham, celery and onion. Equally delicious are seasonal risottos, cooked with asparagus tips, artichoke hearts, fennel, courgettes or pumpkin. Roast-vegetable dishes are popular too.

Sweet Things

Those with a sweet tooth will enjoy *tiramisù* ('pick-me-up'), a creamy, alcoholic coffee and chocolate gâteau. Biscuits, cakes and desserts are a forte, flavoured with spices such as cinnamon and nutmeg. *Fritelle di zucca*, sweet pumpkin doughnut served hot, is a favourite. The best of the renowned ices can be found in *gelaterie* on the **Zattere**.

Wine

The Veneto produces a number of superior (DOC) wines, from the fruity Bardolino to the less prestigious Valpolicella. Soave, the Veneto's

Shopping for Food

For atmosphere as well as fresh ingredients, you can't beat the **Rialto** where you'll find the **Pescheria** – fish market – and the **Erberia** – fruit and vegetable market. Close by, the **Ruga Vecchia di San Giovanni** is full of good food shops. Venetian bakeries throughout the city are a delight. **Rosa Salva**, in Campo Santi Giovanni e Paulo is a celebrated *pasticceria*. Their cakes are wonderful.

Below: a local *enoteca*, or wine bar.

Gay and Lesbian

Except at Carnival time, when anything goes (and it's a wonderful opportunity to be as extravagant, or as anonymous, as you wish), Venice, a conservative city, does not have a lot to offer that is specific to the gay and lesbian community. Many gay people in search of evening entertainment head to the livelier city of Padova about 32 km away, reached by a regular train service. Here are a few recommendations of gay-friendly bars, beaches and hotels along with some practical tips for gay travellers to Venice.

Accommodation

B&B Antico Portego
Rio Terrà Farsetti, Cannaregio 1414/A; tel: 347-495 8326/041-715257; www.bbantico portego.com; vaporetto: San Marcuola; map p.135 C3.
Comfortable accommodation near the railway station, in a beautiful old building with marble pillars and a pleasant courtyard.

B&B Cà del Nobile
Rio Terrà delle Colonne, San Marco 987; tel/fax: 041-528 3473; www.cadelnobile.com; vaporetto: San Marco-Vallaresso; map p.138 B2.

Six spacious, comfortable, antique-furnished rooms in an 18th-century palazzo close to Piazza San Marco.

Venice Villas
Castello 327; tel: 041-570 2834; fax: 041-572 6203; www.venicevillas.it
Venice Villas offers B&B accommodation as well as a finely-restored attic flat in the Palazzo Chittarin Renzovich in the eastern part of the city.

Corte Gherardi Bed & Breakfast
Corte Gherardi, Salizzada S. Cantian, Castello (near the Chiesa dei Miracoli, a short walk

from the Rialto Bridge); tel: 041-523 7376; www.cortegherardi.com; vaporetto: Rialto; map p.135 E1
This Gothic palace has been converted it into one of Venice's most stylish B&Bs, offering a warm welcome and comfortable designer rooms.

Bars/Sauna

Porto de Mar
Via delle Macchine 41–43, Mestre; tel: 041-921 247; www.portodemar.com; closed Mon–Tues
This claims to be the only gay bar in Venice, but it's actually in Mestre, on the mainland (about 15 minutes' walk from Mestre station), not in the historic city. It's good fun, popular with tourists and has themed nights including discos, live music and shows; there's a bus (N1) about every 30 minutes at night if the last train has gone.

Metro Club Saune
Via Cappucina 82b; tel: 041-538 4299; www.metroclub.it; 500 metres from Mestre station
Another gay venue in Mestre,

Below: Dirk Bogarde in Visconti's iconic gay film, *Death in Venice*.

Left: Banner of Arcigay, the national gay organisation.

Magazines

Babilonia was the first gay magazine and is the one with the widest distribution on newsagents' shelves.

Pride is the best-known and can be picked up free in most gay venues in Italy. *Gay Clubbing* is another free listings magazine. In all three publications you can find complete listings of gay and lesbian venues, associations and places offering information on health.

Websites

www.gayfriendlyitaly.com
An excellent website giving information on accommodation, entertainment, beaches, etc., but one that confirms that Venice is not the best place for gays and lesbians to look for friends or entertainment.

www.gay.it
Offers an up-to-date guide (in English and Italian) about gay life throughout Italy.

For holiday reading, take Jeanette Winterson's intriguing novel, *The Passion*. Set during the Napoleonic Wars its features Villanelle, a cross-dressing Venetian woman who can walk on water.

Before you go, hire a DVD and watch (or re-watch) the most iconic gay film with Venetian connections: *Death in Venice*, in which Dirk Bogarde's character suffers silent agonies of love for unobtainable Tadzio.

---

this is a sauna which is frequented by tourists as well as Venetians. An attractive, clean venue, it offers Finnish sauna, Turkish baths, hydromassage, video room, massage (if booked in advance) and a bar with snacks.

As with many of the more upmarket gay venues in Italy, you need to be a member of Arcigay, the national gay organisation, to enter. The Arcicard costs €14, is available at the venue and is valid for one year (www.arcigay.it).

Beaches

Spiaggia Alberoni
Lido di Venezia
From the Lido boat stop, take bus Line B in the direction of Alberoni and go to the end of the line. The gay-naturist section of the beach is to the right of the main entrance.

Spiaggia Isola del Morte
Close to Lido di Jesolo
You can catch a bus from the Piazzale Roma in Venice to the Jesolo bus station in Piazza Drago or – far nicer – a boat from Piazza San Marco (which takes about 40 minutes). From the Jesolo jetty you should head in the direction of Eraclea Mare.

Cruises

The Royal Caribbean Line offers Athens to Venice cruises specifically for gays and lesbians on the *Brilliance of the Seas* (for more information log on to www.mygayweb.com under 'Cruises').

Health

Servizio Igiene e Sanità Pubblica, Via Santa Maria dei Battuti 1B; tel: 041-959 214
For HIV and other health-related information.

Right: Successful lesbian writer, Jeanette Winterson, set one of her best novels in Venice.

History

421	Legendary foundation of Venice on 25 March, conveniently the Feast Day of St Mark.
452–568	Attila the Hun plunders the Veneto. Mass migrations take place from the mainland to Venice.
814	The population moves to the Rivo Alto (Rialto), a more hospitable and easily defended island. Venetian coins first minted. Work begins on the first Doge's Palace.
828	St Mark's body taken from Alexandria to Venice
1000	Venice controls the Adriatic coast. The Marriage to the Sea ceremony is inaugurated in honour of Doge Pietro Orseolo II's defeat of Dalmatian pirates in the Adriatic.
1095–9	Venice joins Crusades, providing ships and supplies for First Crusade to liberate the Holy Land.
1173	First Rialto Bridge begun.
1202–04	The Fourth Crusade; the sack of Constantinople and Venetian conquest of Byzantium provides springboard for the growth of the Venetian empire. The Arsenale shipyards created. Venice emerges as a world power.
1309–10	Work begins on the present Doge's Palace. The Council of Ten is established as a check on individual power and as a monitor of security.
1348–9	A plague outbreak kills half the people of Venice.
1453–4	Constantinople falls to the Turks; zenith of Venetian empire: Treviso, Bergamo, Ravenna, Friuli, Udine and Istria are conquered.
1489	Cyprus ceded to Venice by Queen Caterina Corner.
1508	League of Cambrai unites Europe against Venice. Titian's *Assumption* is hung in the Frari church, Venice. Birth of architect Palladio in the Veneto.
1571	Battle of Lepanto, a decisive naval victory against the Turks.
1577	Palladio designs Il Redentore church.
1669	Loss of Crete, the last major Venetian colony, to the Turks.

5th century: first settlements in the lagoon.

1202–4: *The Sack of Byzantium*, as depicted by Tintoretto.

1271: Marco Polo leaving Venice on his second trip to China.

1501–1521: rule of Doge Loredan, the great diplomat.

1708	A severe winter freezes the lagoon, allowing Venetians to walk to the mainland.
1718	Venice surrenders Morea (Peloponnese) to Turks, signalling loss of its maritime empire; it is left with the Ionian islands and the Dalmatian coast.
1752	Completion of the sea walls.
1790	Opening of La Fenice opera house.
1797	Fall of the 1,000-year-old Venetian Republic. Doge Lodovico Manin abdicates. Napoleon grants Venice to Austria in return for Lombardy.
1800	Papal conclave in Venice to elect pope.
1805–14	Napoleonic rule reinstated.
1815–66	Under the terms of the Congress of Vienna, Austria occupies the city.
1846	Venice joined to mainland by a railway causeway.
1861	Vittorio Emanuele crowned King of united Italy.
1866	Venice annexed to the Kingdom of Italy.
1931	A road causeway connects city to mainland.
1932	First Venice Film Festival takes place.
1945	British troops liberate city from Nazi occupiers.
1960	Construction of the Marco Polo airport.
1966	The worst flood in Venetian history hits the city.
1979	The Venice Carnival is revived.
1988	The first stage of the flood barrier is completed.
1996	Burning down of La Fenice. The worst floods and *acqua alta* (high tides) since 1966.
2003	The Mose (Moses) project gets the go-ahead and work begins on the new mobile flood barrier, due for completion in 2011.
2004	La Fenice opera house finally reopens after reconstruction, with *La Traviata*. Venice gets broadband via fibre-optic cables, dispensing with the need for ugly satellite dishes.
2007	After several years of delay the Ponte Calatrava is constructed across the Grand Canal, linking the railway station with Piazzale Roma.

1496: daily life in 15th-century Venice as captured by Carpaccio.

1571: the Battle of Lepanto.

c. **1900**: a young Eleanor Roosevelt visits Venice.

1996: La Fenice opera house after the fire.

59

Hotels

Venice is the most costly city in Italy and its hotels are notoriously expensive. A simple, central hotel is often the same price as a mid-market hotel elsewhere in Italy. The basic rules when planning your stay are: book early or scan the web for last minute deals, check which way your room faces, and what the price differential is between a tiny room and a palatial room. A hotel may well offer a choice between an expensive large room overlooking the Grand Canal, and a tiny back room overlooking a bleak court-yard. Even so, a room with a view can still cost half as much again as one without a view.

Hotels

Making a choice

The closer you are to **San Marco**, the higher the price of accommodation; with the exception of a few expensive hotels on the **Lido**, **Giudecca** and **San Clemente**. Delightful, central and convenient though the San Marco area is, it feels resolutely touristy, so visitors would do well to broaden their horizons. This can mean choosing somewhere in **Castello**, where the spread of upmarket hotels and newly converted boutique hotels makes it a good choice. Or try an individualistic boutique hotel in the up-and-coming **Cannaregio** area. Although no longer a bargain, the tranquil, romantic **Dorsoduro** district is charming, with small but sought-after mid-market hotels. For families with young children, the Lido makes a good choice, with its sandy beaches and bike rides, but remains the least Venetian area of Venice. The budget alternative is the station area, which is convenient rather than attractive. If forced to stay outside the city, avoid soulless **Mestre** and opt for atmospheric **Padua** or **Treviso**, a 30-minute train ride from Venice.

The euro symbols below are a basic guide for the price per night for a double room with bath or shower, including breakfast, service charge and taxes during high season.

San Marco

Gritti Palace
Campo Santa Maria del Giglio; tel: 041-794 611; fax: 041-520 0942; www.starwoodhotels. com; €€€€; vaporetto: Santa Maria del Giglio; map p.137 E2
Hemingway, Churchill and Greta Garbo all stayed in this 15th-century palace. The most patrician hotel in Venice, it retains the air of a private palazzo, with Murano chandeliers and damask furnishings.

Luna Baglioni
Calle Vallaresso/Calle de l'Ascension; tel: 041-528 9840; fax: 041-528 7160; www. baglionihotels.com; €€€€; vaporetto: San Marco-Vallaresso; P137 E2

Below: Grand Hotel des Bains.

Left: Grand Hotel des Bains, Lido di Venezia.

Flora
Calle della Pergola, off Calle Larga XXII Marzo; tel: 041-520 5884; fax: 041-522 8217; www.hotelflora.it; €€; vaporetto: Santa Maria del Giglio; map p.137 E2

A sought-after, family-run hotel set in a quiet alley near St Mark's. Bedrooms can be palatial or poky (the best are nos. 45, 46 and 47, graced with fin de siècle furnishings). Breakfast in the secluded courtyard garden.

Locanda Art Deco
Calle delle Botteghe; tel: 041-277 0558; fax: 041-270 2891; www.locandaartdeco.com; €€; vaporetto: Sant'Angelo or Accademia; p136 C2

A quiet, good-value hotel in a 17th-century palazzo, just off Campo Santo Stefano, with Art Deco touches.

Locanda Novecento
Calle del Dose; tel: 041-241 3765; fax: 041-520 3721; www.locandanovecento.it; €€; vaporetto: Santa Maria del Giglio; map p.138 B3

An exotic touch of Marrakesh in Venice, with funky Moroccan lamps, and Turkish rugs. There are beamed ceilings, cosy bedrooms and a tiny courtyard for breakfast.

Santo Stefano
Campo Santo Stefano; tel: 041-520 0166; fax: 041-522 4460; www.hotelsantostefano venezia.com; €€; vaporetto:

Prices for an average double room in high season:	
€	under €150
€€	€150–€280
€€€	€280–€500
€€€€	over €500

The oldest hotel in Venice, this was originally a Knights Templar lodge for pilgrims en route to Jerusalem. Set just off Piazza San Marco, it has noble Venetian decor and an 18th-century ballroom plus the grandest breakfast-room in Venice.

Monaco e Grand
Calle Vallaresso; tel: 041-520 0211; fax: 041-520 0501; www.hotelmonaco.it; €€€€; vaporetto: San Marco-Vallaresso; map p.137 E2

A mix of slick contemporary and classic Venetian style. Chic bar and waterfront breakfast room. The hotel's new Palazzo Salvadego annexe is more Venetian.

Saturnia & International
Calle Larga XXII Marzo; tel: 041-520 8377; fax: 041-520 5858; www.hotelsaturnia.it; €€€; vaporetto: Santa Maria del Giglio; map p.137 E2

The mood of this distinctive hotel is vaguely medieval in inspiration which, depending on your mood can be romantic or austere. Bedrooms are intimate and comfortable.

Westin Europa & Regina
Corte Barozzi, off Calle Larga XXII Marzo; tel: 041-240 0001; fax: 041-523 1533; www.westin.com/europaregina; €€€; vaporetto: San Marco-Vallaresso; map p.137 E2

Lovely waterfront position facing La Salute church, this 18th-century palace has been renovated, and the stuccowork and damask tapestries shown off to greater effect. Spacious, bedrooms decorated in Venetian style.

La Fenice et des Artistes
Campiello della Fenice; tel: 041-523 2333; fax: 041-520 3721; www.fenicehotels.it; €€; vaporetto: San Marco-Vallaresso or Santa Maria del Giglio; map p.137 E3

Within a stone's throw of the Fenice opera house, this hotel is popular with singers and musicians; there's a new and an old section, both furnished in traditional style.

VeneziaSi represents over 90 per cent of hoteliers and offers a free booking service (www.veneziasi.it; from abroad, tel: +39-041-522 2264; in Italy, call 199 1733 09). The group also offers hotels on the Lido and on the mainland. Be sure to check that you are actually staying in Venice itself.

Above: Hotel Danieli.

Sant'Angelo or Accademia; map p.137 D2

Set in a 15th-century watch-tower overlooking one of the city's most stylish squares, the hotel has a friendly, unjaded attitude; spa baths throughout; breakfast served on the square.

Castello

Danieli
Riva degli Schiavoni; tel: 041-522 6480; fax: 041-520 0208; www.starwoodhotels.com/danieli; €€€€; vaporetto: San Zaccaria; map p.139 D2

Set on the waterfront, this world-famous hotel has a splendid Gothic foyer, and plush rooms with parquet floors and gilded bedsteads; splendid rooftop restaurant. See also Restaurants p.110.

Londra Palace
Riva degli Schiavoni; tel: 041-520 0533; fax: 041-522 5032; www.hotelondra.it; €€€€; vaporetto: San Zaccaria; map p.139 D2

This elegant hotel has been restored to its old splendour. Tchaikovsky composed his *Fourth Symphony* here in 1877. Comfortable and

civilised with a gourmet restaurant and a lovely terrace; the staff are very welcoming.

Metropole
Riva degli Schiavoni; tel: 041-520 5044; fax: 041-522 3679; www.hotelmetropole.com; €€€€; vaporetto: San Zaccaria; map p.139 D2

Family-owned boutique hotel, renovated and dotted with eclectic antiques and objets d'art. It boasts a Michelin-starred restaurant, trendy bar, lovely garden courtyard and lagoon or canal views; rooms can be cosy (try no. 350) or amusingly kitsch (try no. 251). See also restaurants p.110.

Colombina
Calle del Rimedio; tel: 041-277 0525; fax: 041-277 6044; www.colombinahotel.com; €€€; vaporetto: San Zaccaria; map p.138 C2

Boutique hotel close to St Mark's with a muted, modern take on Venetian style; slick marble bathrooms; balconies with view of the Bridge of Sighs. The new, cheaper annexe is also furnished in traditional style.

Gabrielli Sandwirth
Riva degli Schiavoni; tel: 041-

523 1580; fax: 041-520 9455; www.hotelgabrielli.it; €€€; vaporetto: San Zaccaria; map p.139 D2

Family-run waterfront hotel seemingly mired in a delightful 18th-century time warp; inner courtyard for breakfast, reliable restaurant and panoramic roof terrace.

Liassidi Palace
Ponte dei Greci; tel: 041-520 5658; fax: 041-522 1820; www.liassidipalacehotel.com; €€€; vaporetto: San Zaccaria; map p.139 D2

A boutique hotel in a Gothic palace behind the Riva degli Schiavoni with a muted yet sleek interior; the individualistic bedrooms range from Art Deco to Bauhaus; bar but no restaurant.

Locanda Vivaldi
Riva degli Schiavoni; tel: 041-277 0477; fax: 041-277 0489; www.locandavivaldi.it; €€€;

Prices for an average double room in high season:	
€	under €150
€€	€150–€280
€€€	€280–€500
€€€€	over €500

In recent years Venice has seen a boom in B&Bs (Bed and Breakfasts), providing a cheaper and often more pleasant alternative to a standard tourist hotel. Many of them are in palazzi, often with beautiful furnishings. For information and to book online visit www.venicehotel.com.

vaporetto: San Zaccaria; map p.139 D2

On the lagoon and partially set in the house where Vivaldi once lived. Bedrooms are romantic and individualistic, and many have jacuzzis; breakfast is taken on the roof terrace; Vivaldi's music is often piped into the public rooms.

Palazzo Schiavoni
Fondamenta dei Furlani; tel: 041-241 1275; fax: 041-241 4490; www.palazzoschiavoni.com; €€; vaporetto: San Zaccaria; map p.139 D2

A mix of rooms and apartments in a tasteful new conversion beside the Scuola di San Giorgio, complete with the odd frescoed ceiling; good choice for families.

Santa Marina
Campo Santa Marina; tel: 041-523 9202; fax: 041-520 0907; www.hotelsantamarina.it; €€; vaporetto: Rialto; map p.138 B3

Set between the Rialto and Campo Santi Giovanni e Paolo, this is a pleasant if slightly lacklustre hotel redeemed by friendly, helpful staff; breakfast on the terrace.

Casa Querini
Campo San Giovanni Novo; tel: 041-241 1294/4231; fax: 041-2414231; www.locandaquerini.com; €; vaporetto: San Zaccaria or Rialto; map p.138 C2

Small inn by Campo Santa Maria Formosa with low-key decor, spacious, unexceptional rooms and very pleasant staff.

Locanda La Corte
Calle Bressana; tel: 041-241 1300; fax: 041-241 5982; www.locandalacorte.it; €; vaporetto: Ospedale; map p.138 C3

Small Gothic palace off Campo Santi Giovanni e Paolo; decorated in muted version of traditional Venetian style; inner courtyard for breakfast; bedrooms overlook the canal or the courtyard.

Dorsoduro
Ca' Pisani
Rio Terrà Foscarini; tel: 041-240 1411; fax: 041-277 1061; www.capisanihotel.it; €€; vaporetto: Accademia or Zattere; map p.136 B3

Set in an historic palazzo near the Accademia, this stylish hotel offers a sharp Art Deco design. It has a trendy wine bar/restaurant; all rooms have satellite TV and WiFi connection; a novelty for Venetian hotels.

DD.724
Dorsoduro 724; tel: 041-277 0262; fax: 041-296 0633; www.dd724.it; €€; vaporetto: Salute; map p.137 E1

Named after its address, this is a new, stylish yet welcoming designer hotel close to the Guggenheim; contemporary art complements warm minimalism; flat screen televisions, great breakfasts and willing staff.

Accademia Villa Marevegie;
Fondamenta Bollani; tel: 041-521 0188; fax: 041-523 9152; www.pensioneaccademia.it; €€; vaporetto: Accademia; map p.137 C2

Gracious, highly sought-after wisteria-clad villa at the Grand Canal end of Rio San Trovaso; atmospheric bedrooms and delightful canalside gardens.

Pensione Calcina
Fondamenta Zattere ai Gesuati; tel: 041-520 6466; fax: 041-522 7045; www.lacalcina.com; €€; vaporetto: Zattere; map p.137 C1

Romantic inn, overlooking the Giudecca canal, where art critic John Ruskin lodged in 1876. Charming roof terrace; uncluttered bedrooms (try no. 127); waterside La Piscina dining room and terrace. See also Bars and Cafés p.35.

Below: contemporary comfort.

Prices for an average double room in high season:	
€	under €150
€€	€150–€280
€€€	€280–€500
€€€€	over €500

Ca' San Trovaso

Fondamenta delle Eremite; tel: 041-277 1146; fax: 041-277 7190; www.casantrovaso.com; €; vaporetto: Ca' Rezzonico or San Basilio; map p.136 B2

An unpretentious little hotel on a quiet canal; terracotta floors and damask wallpaper; no television or telephone; roof terrace; ask for room two or four.

Locanda San Barnaba

Calle del Traghetto; tel: 041-241 1233; fax: 041-241 3812; www.locanda-sanbarnaba.com; €; vaporetto: Ca'Rezzonico; map p.135 E2

Small inn near Ca' Rezzonico in a 16th-century frescoed palace run by the ancestral owner; traditional Venetian style; pleasant rooms (ask for frescoed bedroom); canalside courtyard for breakfast.

Cannaregio, San Polo and Santa Croce

Grand Hotel Dei Dogi

Fondamenta Madonna dell'Orto; tel: 041-220 8111; fax: 041-722 278; www.deidogi.boscolo hotels.com; €€€€; vaporetto: Madonna dell'Orto; map p.135 D4

Luxury hotel on the edge of the lagoon; a former monastery that is still an oasis of calm; quiet, tasteful decor; the largest and loveliest hotel garden in Venice.

Ai Mori d'Oriente

Fondamenta della Sensa; tel: 041-711 001; fax: 041-714 209; www.hotelaimoridoriente.it; €€–€€€; vaporetto: Madonna dell'Orto; map p.134 C4

Quirky boutique hotel with lots of character and eclectic and exotic touches, plus welcoming staff.

Bellini

Lista di Spagna; tel: 041-524 2488; fax: 041-715 193; www. bellini.boscolohotels.com; €€€; vaporetto: Ferrovia; map p.134 B2

An upmarket hotel near the station. Set in a refurbished palace overlooking the Grand Canal, with Murano chandeliers in evidence.

Abbazia

Calle Priuli dei Cavaletti; tel: 041-717 333; fax: 041-717 949; www.abbaziahotel.com; €€; vaporetto: Ferrovia; map p.134 A2

Close to the station but tranquil, this former Carmelite foundation has been sensitively restored; beamed ceilings in tasteful bedrooms; courtyard and garden.

Ca' d'Oro

Corte Barbaro; tel: 041-241 1212; fax: 041-241 4385; www.hotel cadoro.it; €€; vaporetto: Ca' d'Oro; map p.135 E2

Set in an historic palazzo near the Ca' d'Oro ferry stop, this quiet, cosy hotel offers a range of rooms from tiny to grand.

Giorgione

Santi Apostoli; tel: 041-522 5810; fax: 041-523 9092; www.hotelgiorgione.com; €€–€€€; vaporetto: Ca' d'Oro; map p.135 E1

Not far from the Ca' d'Oro, this family-run hotel dates back to the 14th century. Decor is traditional Venetian, with chandeliers and Murano glass. The breakfast room opens onto a courtyard; free afternoon coffee and cakes.

Locanda ai Santi Apostoli

Strada Nuova; tel: 041-521 2612; fax: 041-521 2611; www.locandasantiapostoli. com; €€; vaporetto: Ca' d'Oro; map p.135 D2

A discreet family-run inn on third floor of a 14th-century palazzo overlooking the Grand Canal (room 11 has the best view); interconnecting family rooms.

San Cassiano

Calle della Rosa; tel: 041-524 1768; fax: 041-721 033; www.sancassiano.it; €€; vaporetto: San Stae, or Ca' d'Oro via gondola ferry; map p.135 D1

This Grand Canal hotel has much faded charm. Half the rooms have canalside views across to the Ca' d'Oro but vary dramatically in size and price. No lift. Gondola jetty.

Below: rooms with Canalside views come at a price.

Above: nostalgic decor, Hotel Cipriani.

Ca' della Corte
Corte Surian; tel: 041-715 877; fax: 041-722 345; www.cadella corte.com; €; vaporetto: Ferrovia; map p.136 B4
A quiet B&B in a 16th-century palace with private garden and terraces; it offers a variety of accommodation including apartments.

Ca' Gottardi
Strada Nuova; tel: 041-275 9333; fax: 041-275 9421; www.cagottardi.com; €; vaporetto: Ca' d'Oro; map p.135 D2
Overlooking the busy Strada Nuova, this is an elegant and friendly little hotel run by a family of gondoliers.

Ca' Malcanton
Santa Croce 49; tel: 041-710 931 (in the UK 0208 287 8143); www.venice4you.co.uk; €€; vaporetto: San Toma; map p.137 C3
English-owned B&B in a smartly-converted palazzo with a splendid salon and a small canalside garden. Meals on request.

Ca' Pozzo
Sottoportego Ca' Pozzo, Ghetto Vecchio; tel: 041-524 0504; fax: 041-524 4099; www.capozzoinn.com; €; vaporetto: Guglie; map p.134 B3
Small, simple hotel in a modern, minimalist style; pastel hues, exposed beams and modern art.

Locanda Antico Doge
Campo Santi Apostoli; tel: 041-241 1570; fax: 041-244 3660; www.anticodoge.com; €; vaporetto: Ca' d'Oro; map p.135 E1
On a busy but pleasant square; grand breakfast room; damask-draped bedrooms in a palazzo that once housed a doge.

Locanda Leon Bianco
Corte Leon Bianco; tel: 041-523 3572; fax: 041-241 6392; www.leonbianco.it; €; vaporetto: Ca' d'Oro; map p.136 B4
Simple but friendly budget hotel overlooking the Grand Canal entered through a tucked-away courtyard; three of the seven rooms have spectacular canal vistas and are excellent value. Breakfast served in rooms.

Giudecca and San Giorgio Maggiore

Cipriani
Isola della Giudecca 10; tel: 041-520 7744; fax: 041-520 3930; www.hotelcipriani.com; €€€€; vaporetto: Zitelle; map p.22
The Cipriani is the most glamorous of Venetian hotels. Lavish bedrooms are furnished with Fortuny fabrics. There's a pool, gardens and tennis courts, a yacht harbour, and a water-launch that whisks guests to San Marco.

Hilton Molino Stucky
Isola della Giudecca, 753; tel: 041-522 1267; fax: 041-522 1267; www.molinostucky hilton.com; €€€€; vaporetto: Palanca; map p.22
The huge 19th-century flour mill on the Giudecca waterfront has been converted into a 5-star hotel with 380 rooms and Venice's largest congress centre. Facilities include five restaurants and bars, rooftop pool and large spa. The excellent service includes a 'magic' button on the telephone which will summon help for almost anything.

San Clemente Palace
Isola di San Clemente; tel: 041-244 5001; fax: 041-244 5800; www.sanclemente.thi.it; €€€
Romantic hideaway in a converted monastery. Private shuttle from St Mark's; three restaurants, bars, pool, spa and lovely grounds. Luxurious.

Grand Hotel des Bains
Lungomare Marconi, Il Lido; tel: 041-526 5921; fax: 041-526 0113; www.starwoodhotels.com/italy; €€€
Atmospheric Belle Epoque hotel that featured in *Death In Venice*; popular with the stars during the Film Festival; private beach on the Lido.

Locanda Cipriani
Isola di Torcello; tel: 041-730 150; fax: 041-735 433; www.locandacipriani.com; €€
Small, rustic inn in a seemingly remote spot with excellent homely restaurant; run by a branch of the Cipriani family; objets d'art; garden dining.

Quattro Fontane
Via Quattro Fontane, Il Lido; tel: 041-526 0227; fax: 041-526 0726; www.quattrofontane.com; €€
A quirky and much-loved mock-Tyrolean hotel.

There is almost no off-season in Venice so hotels can be fully booked all year. Always book well ahead of peak seasons: Christmas, New Year, Carnival (February), Easter, May, June and September.

Language

I talian is a beautiful language and one that is relatively easy to pick up if you have any knowledge of French (or a grounding in Latin). Most hotels have staff who speak some English, and unless you go well off the beaten track, you should have little problem communicating in shops or restaurants. However, there are places not on the tourist circuit where you will have the chance to practise your Italian, and local people will think more of you for making an effort. It is well worth buying a good phrase book or dictionary but here are a few basics to help you get started.

Pronunciation

Italian pronunciation is fairly straightforward: you pronounce it as it is written. There are a couple of important rules to bear in mind: **c** before **e** or **i** is pronounced **ch**, e.g. *ciao, mi dispiace, la coincidenza*. **Ch** before **i** or **e** is pronounced as **k**, e.g. *la chiesa*. **Sci** or **sce** are pronounced as in sheep or shed respectively. **Gn** is rather like the *ni* sound in onion, while **gl** is softened to resemble the *li* sound in bullion.

Nouns are either masculine (*il*, plural *i*) or feminine (*la*, plural *le*). Plurals of nouns are most often formed by changing an **o** to an **i** and an **a** to an **e**, eg. *il panino: i panini; la chiesa: le chiese*. As a rule, words are stressed on the penultimate syllable unless an accent indicates that you should do otherwise.

Useful Phrases

Yes *Sì*
No *No*
Thank you *Grazie*
Many thanks *Mille grazie/ Tante grazie*
You're welcome *Prego*
All right/That's fine *Va bene*
Please *Per favore* or *per cortesia*
Excuse me (to get attention) *Scusi*
Excuse me (in a crowd) *Permesso*
Could you help me? (formal) *Potrebbe aiutarmi?*
Certainly *Ma, certo/ Certamente*
Can you show me…? *Può indicarmi…?*
Can you help me please? *Può aiutarmi, per cortesia?*
I need… *Ho bisogno di…*
I'm lost *Mi sono perso*
I'm sorry *Mi dispiace*
I don't know *Non lo so*
I don't understand *Non capisco*
Do you speak English/French? *Parla inglese/francese?*
Could you speak more slowly? *Può parlare più lentamente, per favore?*
Could you repeat that please? *Può ripetere, per piacere?*
How much does it cost? *Quant'è, per favore?*
this one/that one *questo/quello*
Have you got…? *Avete…?*

Left: San Marco is the only square to be called a piazza; every other square is a *campo* or tinier *campiello*.

il risotto di mare seafood risotto
le vongole clams
i crostacei shellfish
le cozze mussels
il fritto misto mixed fried fish
i gamberi prawns
il granchio crab
il merluzzo cod
i contorni side dishes
insalata caprese fresh tomato, basil and mozzarella salad

Getting Around

What time do you open/close? *A che ora apre/chiude?*
Closed for the holidays (typical sign) *Chiuso per ferie*
ferry terminal *la stazione marittima*
Where can I buy tickets? *Dove posso fare i biglietti?*
What time does the train/ferry leave? *A che ora parte il treno/vaporetto?*
Can you tell me where to get off? *Mi può dire dove devo scendere?*
Where is the nearest bank/hotel? *Dov'è la banca/l'albergo più vicino?*
right/left *a destra/a sinistra*
Go straight on *Va sempre diritto*

Italian has formal and informal words for 'you'. In the singular, *tu* is informal while *lei* is more polite. For visitors, it is simplest – and safest, to avoid giving offence – to use the formal form.

At a Bar/Restaurant

I'd like to book a table *Vorrei prenotare un tavolo*
Have you got a table for... *Avete un tavolo per...*
I have a reservation *Ho fatto una prenotazione*
lunch/supper *il pranzo/ la cena*
I'm a vegetarian *Sono vegetariano/a*
May we have the menu? *Ci dia la carta?*
What would you like? *Che cosa prende?*
I'd like... *Vorrei...*
a bottle of fizzy/still mineral water *una bottiglia di acqua minerale gasata/ naturale*
red/white wine *vino rosso/ bianco*
beer *una birra*
milk *latte*
pastry/brioche *una pasta*
sandwich/roll

un tramezzino/un panino
the dish of the day *il piatto del giorno*

On the Menu

arrosto roast
al forno baked
alla griglia grilled
involtini stuffed meat rolls
il maiale pork
il fegato liver
il manzo beef
il pollo chicken
affumicato smoked
alle brace charcoal grilled
alla griglia grilled
fritto fried
ripieno stuffed
il pesce fish
il pesce spada swordfish

Below: street scene, Cannaregio.

Literature

Although Venice is associated more closely with art and music than with literature, a great number of writers have lived and worked in the city, fallen in love with it, and made it the subject of novels and poems as well as giving it a major role in their memoirs. Today, writers are still fascinated by the city, either describing its beauties and its idiosyncrasies, or using it as an atmospheric backdrop for stories of mystery, murder and intrigue. Some writers were less than serious about the city. Robert Benchley, on his first visit to Venice, sent a telegram home: 'Streets full of water, please advise'.

Inspirational City

There is something about Venice that seems to get under writers' skins. Among the most famous were the Romantic poet Lord Byron, who occupied several palaces on the Grand Canal at various times and, no respecter of health or safety, often swam its length.

Henry James (1843–1916) may have put his finger on it when he said that 'everyone interesting, appealing, melancholy, memorable or odd' gravitated towards Venice. He used it as the background for two of his most famous novels, *The Wings of the Dove* and *The Aspern Papers*. Charles Dickens was drawn to its seductive decline, and wrote about it in *Pictures from Italy* (1846).

Then there was Mark Twain, entranced by views of the Grand Canal at night, and Marcel Proust, who pondered the passing of time in the Caffè Florian. Ernest Hemingway, a man who propped up many bars, was a regular in Harry's Bar, and stayed in the Locanda Cipriani on Torcello

Above: Henry James was inspired by Venice.

while finishing *Across the River and into the Trees*.

More recently, Ian McEwan, Andrea di Robilant and Sally Vickers have all written 'Venetian novels', and Michael Dibdin and Donna Leon have both created their own Venetian detectives – Aurelio Zen and Guido Brunetti. And that is not even to mention the erudite travel writing by such luminaries as Mary McCarthy and Jan Morris, following in the footsteps of one of the earliest, the diarist John Evelyn, who wrote about the city in the mid-17th century.

Suggested Reading List

Lord Byron, *Childe Harold's Pilgrimage* (1818), classic poetic epic.

John Ruskin, *The Stones of Venice* (1851–53), influential book on the buildings of Venice, for serious lovers of architecture.

Henry James, *The Aspern Papers* (1888) and *The Wings of the Dove* (1902), evocative accounts from one of the greatest observers of Venice.

Mrs Oliphant, *The Makers of Venice* (1898), quirky personal account of Venetian doges, travellers and painters.

Thomas Mann, *Death in Venice* (1912), haunting tale of love and loss.

Ernest Hemingway, *Across the River and into the Trees* (1952), evocative, if not his best.

Mary McCarthy, *Venice Observed* (1961, revised 1982), acerbic look at Venice from an intelligent observer.

Ian McEwan, *The Comfort of Strangers* (1981), an eerie, memorable novel, evocative of the city's melancholic charms.

Left: Byron's room in Palazzo Mocenigo.

This establishment stocks expensive rare and antiquarian books.

Fantoni
Salizzada San Luca, San Marco
The most comprehensive stockist of art books.

Goldoni
Calle dei Fabbri, San Marco (near the Goldoni Theatre)
Large bookshop on two floors, with very helpful staff.

Guggenheim Museum Shop
Palazzo Venier, Dorsoduro
A good selection of books on Venice and Venetian art.

Mondadori
Salizzada San Moisè, San Marco
A cool, central, late-opening bookshop, gallery and multimedia centre with an equally cool bar, Bacaro, attached.

Solaris
Rio Terrà della Maddalena, Cannaregio
Specialises, as the name suggests, in science fiction and fantasy novels.

Tarantola
Campo San Luca, San Marco
Good selection of recent publications; small English-language section.

Christopher Hibbert, *Venice, Biography of a City* (1988), a highly readable and informative survey of the city.

Jan Morris, *Venice* (first published 1960), purple prose meets anecdotal account. *The Venetian Empire: A Sea Voyage,* also by Morris, reconstructs the empire by travelling along the historic Venetian trade routes.

Michael Dibdin, *Dead Lagoon* (1994), a subtle detective story.

Donna Leon, *Friends in High Places* (2001) one of a gritty detective series set in Venice.

Sally Vickers, *Miss Garnet's Angel* (2001), whimsical tale of an art trail in Venice.

Andrea di Robilant, *A Venetian Affair* (2003), an appealing historical romance by an aristocratic Venetian writer.

John Berendt, *The City of Falling Angels* (2005), an intriguing inquiry into mysterious Venice and the lives of its modern residents.

Francesco da Mosto, *Francesco's Venice* (2005), beautifully illustrated history of the city, written by an enthusiastic descendant of the noble da Mosto family.

Bookshops

Libreria Sansovino
Bacino Orseolo, San Marco 84
Specialises in books about Venice.

Libreria Bertoni
Calle della Mandola, San Marco

The style of improvised ensemble theatre known as Commedia dell'Arte originated in Venice: the characters Arlecchino (Harlequin) and Brighella articulated popular sentiment in their never-ending struggle with Pantalone (Pantaloon), the merchant, and Balanzone, the doctor. The genre crystallised into a series of improvisations on stock situations until Carlo Goldoni (1707–93) created a new and more realistic form of Italian comedy. He held a mirror up to his country – and was exiled for his pains.

Right: the miserly merchant, Pantalone, from the Commedia dell'Arte.

Monuments

B uilding in Venice was never easy, but the unique setting inspired generations of architects to produce an eclectic blend of Byzantine, Gothic and Renaissance. The history of Venice can be traced through its monuments. They will lead you from the famous bell tower of San Marco and the proud columns of San Teodoro and San Marco to the state granary, the mint, the salt warehouses, the great houses of the mercantile institutions, the customs house, the iconic city bridges and, of course, the Arsenale, symbol of Venetian maritime power.

When the Campanile collapsed without warning in 1902 the only casualties were the custodian's cat and Sansovino's Classical loggia at the base of the tower, which was completely crushed.

Piazza San Marco

Campanile
Vaporetto: S. Marco Vallaresso/ Giardineti; map p.138 B2

Standing on the site of an earlier watchtower and lighthouse, the bell tower was rebuilt in the 12th century and crowned by a pyramid-shaped spire. During the Republic, each of the bells played a different role, with one summoning senators to the Doge's Palace and another, the execution bell, literally sounding the death knell. The tower collapsed in 1902 but an exact replica was reconstructed. Curiously, although there is a superb view across the city and lagoon from the top, one cannot see the canals.

Columns of San Marco and San Teodoro
Vaporetto: S. Marco Giardinetti; map p.138 C2

The granite columns overlooking the Molo were erected in 1172 and support statues of St Theodore, the city's former patron saint and the Lion of St Mark. While the statue of St Theodore is a modern copy (the original is in the Doge's Palace), the Lion of St Mark is genuine. This ancient winged beast with agate eyes was rescued from Napoleon's clutches in Paris, restored, and returned to his pedestal; this time with a Bible placed under his paw.

La Zecca
Vaporetto: S. Marco Giardinetti; map p.138 B1

This severe 16th-century building, attributed to Sansovino, was the city mint. Venice minted silver and gold ducats from 1284, with the latter known as a *zecchino*, the accepted currency until the fall of the Republic.

Ponte dei Sospiri
Vaporetto: S. Zaccaria Jolanda/ Danieli; map p.138 C2

The famous Bridge of Sighs crosses the canal between the Doge's Palace and the former prisons and courtrooms, allowing interrogators to slip

Above: dungeons in the Doge's Palace.

back and forth. It has two parallel passageways, so that prisoners on their way to be interrogated would not meet those on their way back. The bridge acquired its name after the lamentation of prisoners as they confronted their inquisitors. You can peep into the small, dark cells in which offenders were incarcerated.

Canale Grande

Deposito del Megio
Vaporetto: S. Stae; map p.135 C2

Left: the Rio Canonico and Bridge of Sighs.

sealed off, and the building included a mosque and Turkish baths. The Venetian state insisted that all weapons be surrendered on entry, and forbade Christian women and children from crossing the threshold. The Fondaco only fell into disuse in 1838 and, after an insensitive restoration, became the Museo di Storia Naturale (Natural History Museum). SEE ALSO MUSEUMS AND GALLERIES, P76–7

Quarto Ponte
Vaporetto: Piazzale le Roma; map. p134 1A
The installation of the fourth bridge over the Grand Canal faced years of delay. The €6 million footbridge, designed by the award-winning Spanish architect and engineer, Santiago Calatrava, and created from prefabricated sections, was designed to give a useful connection between Piazzale Roma and the railway station.

> The 'Old Prisons', in the Doge's Palace, where Casanova was once incarcerated, were known as *I Piombi* (The Leads), as they were built directly under the lead roof of the palace.

In San Polo the fortress-like state granary is now a school. The 15th-century building is crenellated, in keeping with the Venetian approach to many public buildings. The Lion of St Mark emblem on the façade is a reconstruction, since Napoleonic troops effaced whatever Republican symbols they found.

Fabbriche Vecchie e Nuove
Vaporetto: Rialto; map p.138 A4
Close to the Rialto stands an arcaded frontage concealing a key pair of mercantile institutions, destroyed by fire in 1514 but rebuilt in Classical style. The ground floors functioned as shops, while the upper floors were administrative offices and courts. Designed by Sansovino, the Fabbriche Nuove is now the Court of Assizes.

Fondaco dei Tedeschi
Vaporetto: Rialto; map p.137 E4
This building, beside the Rialto Bridge, was named after the German merchants who leased the emporium. A healthy trade in precious metals from German mines meant that this privileged community created a cross between an emporium, commercial hotel and social club; it even had its own chapel and casino. After a fire in 1505, it was rebuilt in traditional fashion, with a courtyard and towers that recall an earlier defensive function. The merchants left in 1812, abandoning the site to its banal fate as the city post-office.

Fondaco dei Turchi
Vaporetto: S. Stae; map p.135 C2
Next to the granary the arcaded building in Veneto-Byzantine style was the former trading base for Turkish merchants. It was built in 1227 for the noble Pesaro family but leased to the Ottomans in 1621. Bedrooms, shops and servants' quarters were created. In keeping with Muslim custom, doors and windows were

Below: the Molo from San Marco's campanile.

71

An elegant curve of glass and steel providing a rare splash of architectural modernity in Venice, it is the only bridge to be illuminated at night.

Ponte degli Scalzi
Vaporetto: Ferrovia Scalzi; map p.134 B2

The Bridge of the 'Barefooted' Carmelites, close to the Chiesa degli Scalzi and Santa Lucia station, was constructed in the 1930s, and replaced with one built by the Austrians.

Ponte di Rialto
Vaporetto: Rialto; map p.137 E4; p.138 B3

This was the first bridge to span the Grand Canal, and is the most famous. Earlier wooden bridges on this site collapsed or decayed; this solid stone bridge was constructed in 1588. Picturesque and lined with small shops and souvenir stalls, it is a magnet for visitors.

Castello

Campo dell'Arsenale
Vaporetto: Arsenale; map p.139 E2

The entrance to the naval complex has impressive

The best chance to explore the mysterious Arsenale is during the Biennale, when much of the complex becomes an exhibition space (June–November, odd-numbered years only).

fortifications bounded by 16th-century walls and towers. Beyond the footbridge lies the water entrance, framed by crenellated brick towers, rebuilt in the 17th century. Beside the water gate stands the ceremonial Porta Magna, the majestic land entrance to the Arsenale. Built in 1460, this triumphal arch is celebrated as the first Renaissance monument in Venice. Yet, with typical Venetian eclecticism, the gateway recycles stolen statuary – two lions pillaged from Piraeus, another pair from Delos – as well as four Greek marble columns and their Byzantine capitals.

Ospedaletto
Barbaria delle Tole; Thur–Sat 3.30–6.30pm; vaporetto: Ospedale Civile; map p.139 C3

This cunningly concealed building was one of four

famous *ospedali*, charitable institutions that acted as orphanages and prestigious music conservatoires. The frescoed Sala della Musica formed the main concert hall. It can still be visited during the above hours, but ideally for a concert. The ponderous Baroque façade of the adjoining Ospedaletto church is attributed to Longhena. The church interior is decorated with 17th- and 18th-century paintings, including an early work by Tiepolo.

San Polo

Gobbo di Rialto
Vaporetto: Rialto; map p.138 A4

Campo San Giacomo preserves its mercantile atmosphere, an echo of republican times when money-changers and bankers set up their tables under the church portico. The Hunchback of the Rialto is a curious stooped figure supporting the steps opposite the church. It was on the adjoining pink granite podium, the Pietra del Bando, that republican laws were proclaimed, with the burden borne, literally and

Below: a 6th-century BC lion sits by the Arsenale gateway.

Below: two crenellated towers stand guard at the water entrance to the Arsenale.

Above: gondola repair yard on Rio San Trovaso.

metaphorically, by this figure, a Venetian everyman. Petty criminals were also chased through the streets to the Rialto and were only given sanctuary from the blood-thirsty crowds when they reached these steps.

Dorsoduro

Accademia Bridge
Vaporetto: Accademia; map p.137 D2

This much-loved wooden bridge replaced a cast-iron one rebuilt under the Austrian occupation. An attempt to replace the bridge with a transparent model was defeated by conservative elements although there are now plans to rebuild the decaying wooden version, funded by a commercial sponsor. In a controversial move the bridge will be named after the person who stumps up the cash, at present the leading contenders are billionaires Bill Gates and François Pinault.

Dogana di Mare
Vaporetto: Salute; map p.137 E1

Occupying the triangular tip of Dorsoduro. This was the sea-customs post, as opposed to the land-based customs post (Dogana della Terrà, on the Riva del Vin on the Rialto). Here, ships and cargoes were inspected before being allowed to drop anchor in front of the Doge's Palace. Facing St Mark's Basin, a por-ticoed corner tower is crowned by a rich composi-tion: bronze Atlases bear a golden globe, with a weather-vane featuring the figure of Fortune glinting in the sun. The disused customs house is to be transformed into a gallery, housing contemporary works of art from the collec-tion of François Pinault, the French billionaire who has also acquired the Palazzo Grassi further up the canal.

Magazzini del Sale
Vaporetto: Salute; map p.137 E1

Facing Giudecca island are the former salt warehouses, where the city's sole raw material was stored. The low, Neoclassical frontage con-ceals a 15th-century structure. The interior, an occasional boathouse, also doubles as an exhibition space during the Biennale art festival.

Ospedale degli Incurabili
Vaporetto: Zattere Traghetto; map p.137 D1

On the Zattere, this austere former hospice for syphilitics is a medieval building redesigned by Sansovino in the 16th century. Now a chil-dren's home, in its time it has been an orphanage, a music conservatoire and a barracks.

Squero di San Trovaso
Vaporetto: Zattere; map p.136 C1

On the corner of Rio Trovaso and Rio Ognissanti this pic-turesque gondola repair-yard is best viewed from Fonda-menta Nani on Rio di San Trovaso. Gondolas are over-hauled at one of three *squeri*, traditional boatyards, of which this is the oldest in existence, dating from the 17th century. Naturally, the *squeri* are always set on the waterfront, with the yard slop-ing down to the canal. Beside the boatyard a wooden gal-leried construction, a gera-nium-clad outhouse with living quarters above. The resemblance to an alpine chalet is not accidental: many of the early boat-builders came from the Dolomites.

Over a thousand years ago, the Venetians took the lion as symbol of the city in honour of St Mark. Pacific, playful or warlike, lions pose on flags unfurled over Grand Canal palaces, curl up in mosaics, fly as ensigns above ships, or crouch as statues in secret gardens. A golden winged Lion of St Mark still adorns the city standard.

Museums and Galleries

Venice is rich in artworks and, although many of them are displayed in the churches for which they were painted, or in the *scuole* – confraternities – there is a plethora of galleries and art museums, many of them housed in splendid palaces, displaying works spanning the centuries. There are also museums packed with artefacts relating to Venetian history, archaeology, and specialist collections such as glass and lace. But if you only have time to visit one museum, make it the Accademia, a rich repository of Venetian art.

Venicecard

There is an admission charge for nearly all the museums in Venice, but if you are going to visit a number of them – and use public transport a lot – it may be worth buying an orange Venicecard, which gives you free entry to all the civic museums (the **Musei Civici Veneziani**) as well as free transport.

The civic museums are: the Palazzo Ducale, the Museo Correr, the Torre dell'Orologio (Clock Tower), Ca' Rezzonico, Palazzo Mocenigo, Casa di Carlo Goldoni, Ca' Pesaro, Museo Fortuny, the Museo del Vetro (Glass Museum on Murano), Museo del Merletto (Lace Museum on Burano), the Museo di Storia Naturale (Museum of Natural History) and the Planetario (Planetarium). The card also allows entry to the Museo Ebraico (Jewish Museum), the Fondazione Querini-Stampalia, and 16 churches that belong to Chorus: the Association of Venice Churches.

The cards are not cheap – currently €54.90 full price

Above: these majestic bronze horses, now on view in San Marco's San Marciano Museum, were stolen from Constantinople.

for 48 hours, €46.50 for those aged 29 and under, but can still represent a considerable saving for the culture vulture. See www.venicecard.com and www.museicivicivenezia ni.it for more details.

San Marco

Biblioteca Nazionale Marciana
Piazzetta; tel: 041-240 7211; daily 9am–7pm; combined ticket with the other San Marco museums; access via Museo Correr; vaporetto: Vallaresso-San Marco; p138 B1

A cool, Classical building set in an extended loggia. Designed by Sansovino in 1537, the library is also known as the Libreria Sansoviniana. This long, low building is lined with arches and expressive statues, and graced inside by a sumptuous stairway. Palladio praised it as the richest building since Classical times. The library was designed to house the precious collection of manu-

Left: Supper in the House of Levi, by Veronese (1573) in the Galleria dell' Accademia.

includes coins and battle memorabilia.

The more accessible **picture gallery**, which showcases Venetian art from the 13th to the 16th centuries, may not be a match for the Accademia, but the collection features fine Byzantine-influenced works by Paolo **Veneziano** and Bartolomeo **Vivarini**, and paintings by Giovanni **Bellini**, especially his poignant *Pietà*. The highlight of the museum is **Carpaccio**'s *Two Venetian Ladies* (1507), depicted in a pleasure garden, surrounded by birds and dogs.

Museo Marciano

Basilica di San Marco;
tel: 041-522 5205;
www.basilicasanmarco.it;
Apr–Sep: daily 9.45am–5pm,
Oct–Mar: daily 9.45am–4.45pm;
entrance charge; vaporetto: San

Below: Roman statue of Odysseus in the Archaeological Museum.

Don't be confused by the terminology used on the Venicecard website. When it refers to a 'senior' card it simply means the card for adults over the age of 29, not for senior citizens.

scripts bequeathed by Petrarch in the 14th century, and by Cardinal Bessarion, the Greek humanist, in 1468. The superb **salon** of the original library is covered with paintings by Veronese and Tintoretto.

Museo Archeologico

Piazza di San Marco;
tel: 041-522 5978; daily
8.15am–7.15pm; combined ticket with all the other San Marco museums; entrance is through the Correr Museum 9am–6.30pm, or at no.17 from 8.15am–9am; vaporetto: San Marco-Vallaresso; map p.138 B2
The Museum of Archaeology is housed in part of the Procuratie Nuove and the Biblioteca Marciana. The core collection consists of Greek and Roman sculpture bequeathed by Cardinal Grimani in 1523, which influ-

enced generations of Venetian artists who came to draw and study here. Among the Roman busts, medals, coins and cameos are Greek originals and Roman copies, including a 5th-century Hellenistic *Persephone*.

Museo Correr

Piazza di San Marco, Ala Napoleonica; tel: 041-240 5211; daily 9am–7pm; combined ticket with the other San Marco museums; vaporetto: San Marco-Vallaresso; map p.138 B2
This often overlooked museum of Venetian civilisation is housed in the Procuratie Nuove, with the entrance in the Ala Napoleonica; the Napoleonic Wing. The **Neoclassical rooms** make a fitting setting for Canova's sculptures. The first section is a romp through Venetian history, featuring representations of the Lion of St Mark, and paintings of festivities and ceremonies. The final historical section covers the troubled times from the fall of the Republic to French and Austrian domination, and

Above: Ca' Rezzonico, a Baroque masterpiece on the Grand Canal, is home to the Museum of 18th-Century Venetian Life.

Marco-Vallaresso; map p.139 B2
To reach the Museo Marciano, take the steep narrow steps up from the Basilica di San Marco, as the museum is in the gallery above the entrance portal. From here, you get views over the piazza and into the basilica itself.

The main reason to visit, however, is to see the Classical **horses** that formerly adorned the façade of San Marco, symbolising the Venetian Republic's untrammelled independence. The rearing animals were brought to Venice as Byzantine booty: they had previously stood on a triumphal arch in Rome before gracing the hippodrome in Constantinople. When Napoleon invaded Venice he took them to Paris where they remained for 18 years; they were returned to Venice in 1815. Despite the demise of the Republic, the prancing horses are still proud, and remain the only team pulling a chariot to survive from Classical times.

The Grand Canal

Galleria d'Arte Moderna
Ca' Pesaro, Santa Croce; tel: 041-524 0695; daily Apr–Oct: 10am–6pm, Nov–Mar: 10am–5pm; combined ticket with the Museo d'Arte Orientale; vaporetto: San Stae; map p.134 A3
The Gallery of Modern Art occupies part of Ca' Pesaro, a stately Baroque pile that the Duchess Bevilacqua La Masa bequeathed to the city in 1899. This is a slick showcase for modern art (although the coffered and frescoed ceilings also merit admiration).

A **sculpture-lined court-yard** leads upstairs to the museum, past one of Rodin's quizzical *Thinkers*. The early rooms contain pastoral paintings by the

Tuscan Impressionists and works by early winners of the Biennale. The grand *portego*, or ceremonial salon, displays the show-stoppers, from Klimt's decadent *Salome* and Chagall's *Rabbi of Vitebsk* to Bonnard's *Nude in the Mirror* and Lavery's *Woman in Pink*. Later rooms focus on the Italians, from Morandi to De Chirico and Carlo Carra.

Museo di Storia Naturale
Fondaco dei Turchi, Salizzada del Fontego, Santa Croce; tel: 041-275 0206; Tue–Fri 9am–1pm, Sat–Sun 10am–4pm; free; vaporetto: San Stae; map p.134 C2
The museum is housed in the Fondaco dei Turchi. The collection includes the sarcophagi of previous doges; the one bearing no inscription belonged to the disgraced Marin Faliero, the doge decapitated for treason in 1355. The museum has been refurbished, but only the aquarium and dinosaur sections are open, along with an

> The writer Jan Morris mourned the fate of the Classical horses, 'the supreme talismans of Venetian power... chafing their gilded hooves in the humiliation of decline'.

interesting ecological presentation on the lagoon's fauna and flora.

Museo d'Arte Orientale
Ca' Pesaro; tel: 041 524 1173; daily Apr–Oct: 10am–6pm, Nov–Mar: 10am–5pm; combined ticket with the Galleria d'Arte Moderna; vaporetto: San Stae; map p.135 E2

The Museum of Oriental Art is housed in Ca' Pesaro, along with the Galleria d'Arte Moderna *(see previous page)*. The museum draws on the eclectic 19th-century collection assembled by the Count di Bardi on his travels to the Far East. Japanese art of the Edo period (1614–1868) is mixed with oriental decorative screens and lacquerwork. There are also precious fabrics, musical instruments, costumes and armour, plus masks and puppets. While the fate of this somewhat fusty time capsule is uncertain, it remains an endearing collection.

Museo del Settecento Veneziano
Ca' Rezzonico; tel: 041-241 0100; Wed–Mon 10am–6pm; entrance charge; vaporetto: Ca' Rezzonico; map p.136 C3

The rococo interior of Ca' Rezzonico has been sumptuously restored in recent years, with the re-hung picture gallery of superior genre-artists on the second floor, and the eclectic art gallery on the top floor, together forming the **Museum of 18th-Century Venetian Life**. A grand staircase leads to the Piano Nobile, an opulent setting for Tiepolo's trompe l'oeil ceilings and Guardi's memorable genre scenes. The **Sala da Ballo**, or ballroom, is boldly restored, daringly frescoed and richly embellished with glittering chandeliers and period pieces, including ebony vase-stands borne by Moors.

Off the ballroom is the **Sala dell'Allegoria Nuziale** (1758), raised to great heights by Tiepolo's nuptial allegory on the ceiling, ostensibly depicting *The Marriage of Ludovico Rezzonico*. Accompanied by angels and cherubs, careering horses tumble through the billowing heavens, forging a link between the elevated residents and the gods. In the same year, a Rezzonico count was elected pope, thus putting the seal on the family's social supremacy. Elsewhere there are lofty Tiepolo frescoes depicting *Nobility and Virtue* and *Fortitude and Wisdom*.

After recent renovation,

Above: *People with Masks*, by Pietro Longhi (1760) in the Ca' Rezzonico museum.

the second floor rivals the Piano Nobile in magnificence, with the huge *portego* used as a picture gallery for genre scenes by **Canaletto**, **Guardi** and **Longhi**. Genre painters seems a disparaging term for these great 18th-century salon artists at the peak of their powers.

Guardi's *Ridotto* (1748) captures the revelry of masked gamblers and revellers in the state casino, while his *Nuns' Parlour* (1768) depicts the spirited and worldly nuns whose reputation for lasciviousness made Venetian convents a byword for dissolute living. Longhi's superior salon pictures show patrician Venice at play, including the famous *Rhinoceros Show,* depicting masqueraders entranced by this exotic beast.

Also on display is one of the few works by Canaletto in Venice: his view of the *Rio dei Mendicanti* (1725). There are also subtle paintings and miniatures by Rosalba Carriera, the 18th-century portraitist.

Apart from these genre scenes and **Tiepolo's frescoed ceilings**, the highlight

Below: *Nobility and Virtue triumphing over Perfidy*, a fresco by Tiepolo in the Ca' Rezzonico.

is the suite of rooms dedicated to frescoes salvaged from Villa Zianigo, the Tiepolo family home. Giandomenico Tiepolo's provocative yet playful frescoes reveal the mood of disenchantment in Venice towards the end of the 18th century. The greatest of these strange and unsettling pictures is *Mondo Nuovo* (New World), depicting a crowd staring out to sea, and suggesting the disorientation created by the fall of the Venetian Republic, with Venetians reduced to being mere bystanders.

If the second floor is a fond farewell to the Serenissima, the **top floor** is a tribute to the taste of one of Venice's most renowned art patrons, Egidio Martini. This well-displayed private collection spans four centuries of northern Italian art, including works by Tintoretto and

Tiepolo. But its appeal lies in the collection's eclectic nature, fashioned by one man's singular tastes. Here, too, is a quaint period pharmacy, complete with ceramic jars, glass bottles and wooden cabinets.

Galleria Franchetti

Ca' d'Oro; tel: 041-523 8790; www.artive.arti.beniculturali.it (Italian only); Mon 8.15am–2pm, Tue–Sun 8.15am–7.15pm; entrance charge; vaporetto: Ca' d'Oro; map p.135 D2

This venue is one of the most appealing of the city's art galleries. If the collection is idiosyncratic, it reflects the refined taste of the owner.

The gallery is adorned with Flemish tapestries as well as Gothic and Renaissance furniture. The highlights of the collection include a delightful *Annunciation* by Carpaccio, Guardi's views of Venice and Titian's

> The *portego* (gallery) in the Galleria Franchetti opens onto the Grand Canal; from the loggia, looking towards the Rialto, there is a splendid view of the *pescheria*, the fish market.

Venus. Andrea Mantegna's *St Sebastian* is the most poignant of his paintings, with other versions existing in Paris and Vienna: this was Franchetti's favourite work. Yet it is the minor Venetian works that give the greatest pleasure, ranging from 12th-century sculptures of interlaced peacocks to Vivarini's poetic Byzantine-style paintings.

A wooden Gothic staircase leads to the top floor. This contains minor works by leading Venetians, including fragments of frescoes by Giorgione and Titian which once adorned the exterior of the Fondaco dei Tedeschi on the Grand Canal. These were removed for preservation.

Peggy Guggenheim Collection

Palazzo Venier dei Leoni, Dorsoduro; tel: 041-240 5411; www.guggenheim-venice.it; Wed–Mon 10am–6pm; entrance charge; vaporetto: Accademia or Salute; p138 B2

Housed in the 18th-century Palazzo Venier, the collection is named after the American millionairess, art collector and benefactor who lived here from 1949 until her death 30 years later. It is appropriate that this startlingly modern-looking building should house a superb collection of modern art.

This is a deservedly popular showcase for

Left: Promotional poster produced by the Italian State Railway (1900) in the Ca' d'Oro.

Above: Palazzo Venier dei Leoni, home of the Peggy Guggenheim Collection of modern art. The uncharacteristically low building is known as the 'Nonfinito' - Unfinished.

Chagall, Dalí, Klee, Braque, Giacometti, Kandinsky, Bacon and Sutherland. Most major movements are represented in the gallery, from Picasso's **Cubist** period to Severini's **Futurism**; from Mondrian's abstract works to **Surrealist** masterpieces by De Chirico, Delvaux and Magritte. Max Ernst, Guggenheim's second husband, is well represented.

Other highlights include De Chirico's *Red Tower*, Magritte's *Empire of Light* and Pollock's *Alchemy*, forming a complement to the new collection in Ca' Pesaro.

Although Peggy Guggenheim helped launch American artist Jackson Pollock, there is little Expressionist work here, since it did not find favour with the otherwise discerning collector.

The **sculpture-lined gardens** feature works by Henry Moore and Marino Marini, and new pieces continue to be acquired. The water gates are often closed, to conceal the provocative erection sported by the rider in Marini's *Angel of the Citadel*.

Castello

Fondazione Querini-Stampalia

Calle Querini; tel: 041-271 1411; Tue–Sun 10am–6pm, Fri–Sat 10am–10pm; entrance charge; vaporetto: San Zaccaria; map p.138 C3

This is one of the best small galleries in Venice, intimate, eclectic and uncrowded. The

Below: Marini's provocative *Angel of the Citadel*, in the courtyard of the Guggenheim Museum.

Querini belonged to the ancient nobility, the families who elected the first doge. However, a foiled plot led to the dynasty's banishment to the Greek island of Stampalia, a title they later appended. The last count died in 1868 and bequeathed his home to the city.

Count Giovanni left his stamp on this Renaissance palace, from the new library to the gallery hung with family portraits and Venetian paintings, mainly 17th- and 18th-century genre scenes. Highlights include a poetic Bellini painting and the festive and domestic scenes of Gabriele Bella (1730–99). Several famous works by Longhi include T*he Geography Lesson* and *The Ridotto,* depicting masqueraders at the casino. The count's taste in furniture is typical of the refined yet relatively spartan interiors favoured by the nobility.

Given such pared-down chic, it is fitting that the ground floor was remodelled by Carlo Scarpa, the Venetian

79

Above: *View of the Island of Corfu,* by an unknown Italian painter (1700) in the Museo Storico Navale .

Modernist architect, in the 1960s, creating an airy atrium and a **Japanese minimalist garden**. Evening classical concerts are held in the frescoed **main salon** while the chic café is also highly recommended.

Museo Diocesano di Arte Sacra

Ponte della Canonica; tel: 041-522 9166; Mon–Sat 10.30am–12.30pm; free, with donation; vaporetto: San Zaccaria; map p.138 C2

The Museum of Sacred Art is tucked away behind the Doge's Palace and Riva degli Schiavoni. The Romanesque cloisters of this canalside museum form an oasis of calm amid the bustle of San Marco. Ranged around the cloisters are fragments of early medieval sculptures from San Marco, as well as Roman and Byzantine statuary. The museum displays works salvaged from deconsecrated churches, along with Mannerist and Baroque art.

Museo Dipinti Sacri Bizantini

Rio dei Greci (near San Giorgio dei Greci church); tel: 041-522 6581; Mon–Sat 9am–4.30pm, Sun 10am–5pm; entrance charge; vaporetto: San Zaccaria; map p.139 D2

The Museum of Sacred Byzantine Art is housed in the former Greek *scuola*, or confraternity house, now run by the Hellenic Institute. The confraternity chapter house has kept its Baroque decor, while the museum displays an outstanding collection of 16th- and 17th-century Cretan works, which illustrate the synthesis of Greek and Venetian art.

Museo Storico Navale

Riva San Biagio; tel: 041-520 0276; Mon–Fri 8.45am–1.30pm, Sat 8.45am-1pm; entrance charge; vaporetto: Arsenale; map p.139 E1

Given the elusiveness of the Arsenale, the Naval Museum is the only place where you can fully appreciate the greatness of maritime Venice. Before its present incarnation, the 16th-century building was used as a naval granary and biscuit warehouse. The Austrians created the collection from the scant

At the entrance to the Ghetto, **Gam Gam** (tel: 041-715 284, closed Fri–Sat) is the only kosher restaurant in Venice, and specialises in Italian-Jewish and Ashkenazi dishes.

remnants to survive French depredations. (Many Venetian naval treasures are now displayed in the rival Parisian naval museum.)

The museum is considerably more spacious than it first appears, so you may wish to restrict your visit to the lower floors; the **top floor** is devoted to uniforms, pennants and insignia. Apart from naval maps and nautical instruments, the collection includes a range of weaponry, from 17th-century breech-loaders to heavy cannons and World War II torpedoes. The Venetian antiquarian maps depict the development of the Arsenale and the lagoon defences, while Venetian naval supremacy is illustrated by scenes of naval battles such as Lepanto, and by models of Mediterranean fortresses.

Venetian shipyards generally built boats from models rather than drawings. Models on display range from early Egyptian and Phoenician craft to Greek triremes and a Venetian galley. Gondolas naturally play a prominent role, including the original ones equipped with a *felze*, the wooden cabin that protected passengers from

Above: *Mary with Child and Saints*, by Bellini (1504) in the Galleria dell' Accademia.

prying eyes and winter weather. One of the main highlights is a scale model of the last **Bucintoro**, the legendary State barge – a sumptuous, gilded vessel used by the doge.

Cannaregio

Museo della Comunità Ebraica

Campo del Ghetto Nuovo; tel: 041-715359; Oct–May: Sun–Fri 10am–5.30pm, June–Sept: Sun–Fri 10am–7pm; guided tours of the synagogues every hour from 10.30am–4.30pm (from 1 June to 5.30pm) in Italian and English; entrance charge; vaporetto: San Marcuola; map p.134 B3

The Jewish Museum chronicles life in the Ghetto, and there are tours of the synagogues every hour from 10.30am to 4.30pm. The hinges of the former Ghetto gates can be seen on Sottoportego Ghetto Nuovo, evoking a drawbridge leading to a mysterious world.

Dorsoduro

Galleria dell'Accademia

Campo della Carità; tel: 410-522 2247; www.artive.arti.benicult urali.it (Italian only); Mon 9am–2pm, Tue–Sun 8.15am–7.15pm; entrance charge; vaporetto:

Accademia; map p.137 C2

This treasury of Venetian art ranges from Renaissance masterpieces and Byzantine panel paintings to vibrant ceremonial paintings, grand tour caprices and even portraiture. Yet it remains intimate rather than overwhelming, as memorable for its revealing snapshots of everyday life as for its masterpieces.

The core collection was assembled by Venetian

artists themselves in the 18th century. Since the gallery is lit by natural light, choose a bright day to explore this vaguely chronological collection of art works dating from the 14th to 18th centuries. Highlights include intimate works by **Carpaccio** and Giovanni **Bellini**, High Renaissance art by **Giorgione**, **Titian**, **Tintoretto** and **Veronese**, and genre scenes by **Tiepolo**, **Guardi** and **Canaletto**.

Room I occupies the Gothic chapter house, and is dedicated to Byzantine and Gothic artists. **Rooms II to IV** display expressive early Renaissance altarpieces by Giovanni Bellini. **Room V** showcases further masterpieces by Bellini and the gallery's most celebrated work: Giorgione's *The Tempest* (*c.* 1507), a moody and enigmatic canvas. Beside it, *The Old Woman*, by the same artist, is a striking piece of early realism.

Rooms VI to X feature Renaissance and Mannerist

Below: *Meeting of the young Veronese with Titian*, by Antonio Zona (1861), in the Galleria dell' Accademia.

masters, from Titian to Veronese and Tintoretto. Titian's poignant *Pietà*, intended for his own tomb, is lit by a diffuse light. Also here is Tintoretto's *Miracle of the Slave*, the work that made his reputation.

Rooms XII to XVII display 18th-century landscapes and genre paintings. **Room XIX to the end**, return to the Renaissance, with a showcase of the pomp and pageantry of the Venetian Republic. The last room displays Titian's *Presentation of the Virgin*, painted for this very room.

Above: *Presentation of the Virgin at the Temple*, by Titian, in the Galleria dell' Accademia.

The Islands

There are not many museums on the lagoon islands, but a few places worth visiting are listed below.

SAN GIORGIO MAGGIORE
San Giorgio Maggiore Fondazione Cini
Some sections can be viewed during exhibitions, but for a full

Below: *Minerva and the Four Cardinal Virtues* (1665), a ceiling painting in San Giorgio Maggiore.

tour call the foundation: tel: 041-271 0228; vaporetto: San Giorgio Maggiore; map p.22
The island of San Giorgio Maggiore and the **monastic complex** of the Benedictine church of the same name, were rescued from a century-long period of decline by Count Vittorio Cini (1884–1977).

Highlights are the huge Renaissance **dormitory** and the cross-vaulted Palladian **refectory**. More impressive still are the Renaissance **Chiostro degli Allori** (Cloister of the Laurels) and the Palladian **Chiostro dei Cipressi** (Cloister of the Cypresses). Palladio also designed the ceremonial guest quarters overlooking the lagoon. The sumptuous setting is more reminiscent of a palace courtyard than of a cloistered retreat. The cloisters lead to the monastic gardens and the **Teatro Verde**, where open-air opera performances are staged.
SEE ALSO MUSIC, P.84

MURANO
Museo del Vetro
Fondamente Giustinian 8, tel: 041-739 586; Apr–Oct: Thur–Tue 10am–5pm, Nov–Mar: Thur–Tue 10am–4pm; entrance charge; vaporetto: Museo; map p.24
The Glass Museum occupies the Gothic Palazzo Giustinian, originally the seat of the bishop of Torcello, which transferred here after the earlier settlement was abandoned. Although the palace retains a few original frescoes, it is now essentially a showcase for **Murano glass**, from platters and beakers to crystal chalices and the finest chandeliers. Non-Venetian pieces include a Roman mosaic bowl, matched by mosaics from the local church of Santi Maria e Donato. As well as Renaissance enamelled glassware, there are satirical scenes mocking the Austrian rulers, Art Nouveau objets d'art, and the glittering blue Coppa Barovier, a Gothic wedding chalice, adorned with allegorical love scenes.

BURANO
Museo del Merletto
Piazza Galuppi; tel: 041-730 034; Wed–Mon 10am–4pm; entrance charge; vaporetto: Burano; map p.24
The museum is housed in a Gothic palace, which was formerly the lace school, in

the town square. Given the difficulties of preserving lace, most samples on display tend to be from the 19th century, including a fine wedding train. Lace has been made in Venetian convents since medieval times, but the *punto in aria* method, using a needle and thread, only emerged in the 16th century. The art fell into decline with the Industrial Revolution, but was saved from extinction on Burano by the creation of a lacemaking school in 1872. By the turn of the 19th century, the industry sustained 5,000 people, but factory-made lace also fell out of fashion.

LAZZARETTO NUOVO
Lazzaretto Nuovo monastery
Visits by prior arrangement only, through Archeo Venezia, tel: 041-520 6713.
This austere island was a Benedictine monastery complex until 1468, when it became a quarantine centre for Venetian ships suspected of harbouring contagion.

> The island of Lazzaretto Nuovo was dubbed 'new' *(nuovo)* to distinguish it from Lazzaretto Vecchio, off the Lido, the 'old' quarantine island for plague victims.

Designed to combat the spread of diseases transported via oriental ports, the island became a model for quarantine centres all over the Mediterranean, from Malta to Marseilles. In Austrian times, the island was converted into a military garrison, with a gunpowder and munitions factory. The most impressive building is the Teson Grande, a barn-like 16th-century structure, complete with historical graffiti.

SAN LAZZARO
San Lazzaro degli Armeni
Tel: 041-526 0104; daily 3.20-5pm (guided visits); entrance charge; vaporetto 20 from San Zaccaria at 2.45pm
A former leper colony, the island was given to the Armenians in 1717 and today is a scholarly Armenian centre.

The setting is idyllic with the church and cloisters surrounded by orchards, gardens and strolling peacocks. Guided tours cover the church, cloister, picture gallery, museum, a library of priceless books and manuscripts and an ancient printing press which was capable of reproducing 36 languages. One room is dedicated to Byron who came here to learn Armenian and assist in the research of an Armenian-English dictionary.

TORCELLO
Museo del Estuario
Palazzo del Consiglio; tel: 041-730 761; Apr–Oct: Tue–Sun 10.30am–5pm, Nov–Mar: Tue–Sun 10am–4.30pm; combined ticket with basilica and campanile; vaporetto: Torcello
Exhibits include mosaics from Ravenna and fragments from Torcello's *Last Judgement*, lost during a clumsy restoration in 1853. Compared with the largely intact original buildings, these are the broken shards of a lost civilisation.

Below: Murano Glass, 1950s.

Music

Venice is a deeply musical place, and many of the sounds of the city are free: visitors wandering the canals will often hear music students practising their Chopin or Schubert. Vivaldi, Monteverdi and Wagner lived in Venice, and concerts of Vivaldi's music are staged regularly in churches. And, of course, there's opera at La Fenice. The city is less well-known for jazz and contemporary music, which often tends to be confined to bars, but the scene is getting better. The most popular venues for classical-music concerts, from organ recitals to choral works, are Venice's many churches and the *scuole* (confraternities).

Monteverdi and Vivaldi

The 17th and 18th centuries were the golden age of Venetian music, celebrated by Vivaldi and Monteverdi. Claudio Monteverdi (1567–1643) is regarded as the founder of Venetian opera, but to contemporary critics Venetian violin virtuoso Antonio Vivaldi (1678–1741) is one of the most important composers of late Baroque music.

Church Concerts

Classical concerts are held in the vast Gothic church of I Frari; in Tintoretto's church of **Madonna dell'Orto**, and in the basilica of **La Salute**. The Renaissance church of **Santa Maria dei Miracoli**, the Rialto market church of **San Giacometto**, the neighbourhood **Santa Maria Formosa** church, the church of **La Pieta** and the deconsecrated **Church of San Vidal** are also evocative settings for concerts.

On Piazzetta dei Leoncini (St Mark's Square), the **Ateneo San Basso** (tel: 041-521 0294) is the setting for concerts of Vivaldi's and Mozart's works.

SEE ALSO CHURCHES, P.38–45

Confraternity Concerts

The **Scuola Grande di San Teodoro** (Campo San Salvador, San Marco; tel: 041-521 8294) stages concerts, with singers and orchestra in 18th-century costume. Concerts are also held in the splendidly decorated confraternity houses of **Scuola Grande di San Rocco**, **Scuola Grande dei Carmini**, **Scuola Grande di San Giovanni Evangelista** and the **Ospedaletto**.

Opera

Opera in Venice has a rather tragic history. The city's main opera house, **La Fenice** (The Phoenix), once dubbed 'the prettiest theatre in Europe', was badly damaged by fire in 1996 – its third fire since its construction in 1774. It reopened after restoration in 2004. The theatre stages ballet and concerts as well as opera.

La Fenice
Campo San Fantin, San Marco; tel: 041-24 24; www.teatro

Above: Antonio Vivaldi, the 'red-haired priest'.

lafenice.it; vaporetto: S. M. del Giglio; map p.137 E2
The opera season runs from September–June.

Teatro Malibran
Campiello Malibran, Cannaregio 5873; tel: 041-786 601; vaporetto: Rialto; map p.138 B4
Another attractive venue for opera is this tiny jewel of a theatre that reopened in 2001 after 10 years of restoration.

Teatro Verde
Isola di San Giorgio Maggiore, tel: 900 800 800; www.teatro verde.de; map p.22

Left: inside La Fenice, one of Italy's best-known opera houses.

If you don't manage to get tickets for La Fenice but would like to see inside this famous opera house, there are now guided tours in five languages. The 45-minute tours normally take place daily but times vary. Telephone reservations are required (tel: 041-24 24).

Osteria Ruga Rialto
Ruga Rialto; tel: 041-521 1243; vaporetto: Rialto; map p.137 E4
This venue offers live jazz, blues and reggae.

Paradiso Perduto
Fondamenta della Misericordia; tel: 041-720 581; vaporetto: Fer. Bar Roma; map p.134 B2
A large, boisterous bar, with live jazz, folk and ethnic music, open til 1am nightly (2am on Saturdays).

Pizzeria 900 Jazz Club
Campiello dei Sansoni, San Polo; tel: 041-522 6565; vaporetto: Rialto; map p.135 D1
Intimate popular club, with Italian and international live jazz. Good pizzas too.

Outdoor Concerts

In summer, some of the squares in Dorsoduro, including Campo Pisani, are turned into open-air concert venues.

To book tickets for opera, concerts, ballet and other events, contact **HelloVenezia** (tel: 041-24 24; www.hellovenezia.it; open 7.30am–8pm). There are HelloVenezia agencies at Piazzale Roma, the railway station and on the Lido.

This open-air amphitheatre on the island of San Giorgio Maggiore reopened in 2007 to stage Strauss' operetta *A Night in Venice*.

Other Venues

Concerts are also staged in the city's greatest palaces, from **Ca' Vendramin-Calergi** (usually Wagner) to **Ca' Rezzonico** (18th-century music) and the **Palazzo Barbarigo-Minotto** (opera arias) overlooking the Grand Canal.

The **Querini-Stampalia** (tel: 041-271 1411) is a small gallery providing an intimate yet sumptuous setting for evening and lunchtime recitals. La Fenice (see p.84 for details) stages symphonic concerts and chamber recitals as well as opera. Ai Musicanti, the concert cafè, staging operatic highlights and famous Italian melodies from April to October, has reopened in a new venue at **Campo San Gallo**, San Marco (www.ai-musicanti.com).

Jazz & Contemporary

Teatro Fondamenta Nuove
Fondamenta Nuove, Cannaregio 5013; tel: 041-522 4498; www.teatrofondamentanuove.it; vaporetto: Celestia; map p.139 E3
Contemporary and experimental music, from jazz to multi-media projects.

Below: look out for posters advertising forthcoming concerts.

Nightlife

Traditionally, nightlife in Venice has tended to be low-key, focused on piano bars, the historic cafés around San Marco, and chic hotel bars. The average night out revolves around a restaurant meal preceded or rounded off with a cosy aperitif or cocktail, and a stroll before bed. But Venetians of all ages have become far more adventurous of late. By diversifying the bar scene, revamping the top hotel bars, opening stylish designer bars, and bringing the *bacaro* (wine bar) concept up to date, Venice has surruptitiously acquired a burgeoning new nightlife scene.

Setting the Scene

The best nightspots, excluding the grand hotel bars, are as popular with Venetians as with visitors, and the age range is decidedly mixed, too. If romance and glamour are the goals, then the waterfront-hotel piano bars possess it in abundance. If elegant designer bars, jazz or lounge-music clubs appeal, then most are within walking distance of St Mark's.

If you want to sample some of the reinvented *bacari*, new spins on the traditional Venetian bars, then slip off to quiet *campi* and *calli* in Castello, San Polo or Dorsoduro.

The cocktail hour between 7pm and 8pm is a Venetian ritual: the locals can be seen sipping wine or classic cocktails in chic cafés or old-fashioned neighbourhood bars. But even in the stylish new venues you can still request *un'ombra* (literally a shadow), a tiny and inexpensive glass of white Veneto wine, downed in one go.

Given the middle-aged Venetian population (the average age is 45), the historic centre of Venice has no recommended dance venues – only a few staid and distinctly old-fashioned nightclubs and a couple of 'disco-clubs'.

Many young Venetians dance the night away with tourists in the clubs on the **Lido di Jesolo** on the Adriatic coast. (But you will need to get a taxi, taking a road with a high accident rate. There are buses and ferries, but they do not run late at night.)

In the summer, the nightlife scene switches to the **Venice Lido**, and focuses on the seafront and the grand hotels.

The following nightlife options are presented by area. Fortunately, if you don't feel like straying far from **San Marco**, the most romantic spots tend to be nearby, with the top hotel bars overlook-

Venice is noted for its cocktails, especially the Bellini *(right)*, the delicious aperitif of fresh peach juice and sparkling Prosecco. But to look like a Venetian, risk the lurid orange cocktail known as a spritz. Introduced to Venice during the Austrian occupation, it consists of roughly equal parts of dry white wine, soda water and an aperitif, usually Campari or Aperol.

For traditional Venetian haunts, try the alleys off Strada Nuova (especially the Campo Santi Apostoli end) in Cannaregio, which conceal some excellent *bacari*.

ing the waterfront on Riva degli Schiavoni or the Grand Canal.

However, the **Dorsoduro** area covers some of the most charming spots, ranging from classic cocktail-bars to tastefully gentrified wine-bars, as well as a lot of new places around Campo Santa Margherita, aimed at a brasher, younger crowd.

Cannaregio, meanwhile, favours more idiosyncratic nightlife, from the best of traditional wine bars (*bacari*) to eclectic music clubs and ethnic haunts that are satisfyingly diverse for such a conservative city. Even so, bear in mind that the hottest spots are often tucked away down labyrinthine alleys.

Right: Piazza San Marco at Carnival time.

Clubs and Bars

SAN MARCO
Torino@notte
Campo San Luca; tel: 041-522 3914; closed Sun; vaporetto: Rialto; map p.138 A2
A youthful late-night drinking den.

Centrale
Piscina Frezzeria, off Frezzeria; tel: 041-296 0664; daily 7pm–2am; vaporetto: Rialto; map p.137 E3
An inviting haunt for nightowls of all ages. Set in a converted cinema, itself carved out of an ancient palazzo, this stylish lounge bar is moody and modern, a great place for cocktails or dinner.

Left: the trendy Bacaro Lounge in San Marco.

Harry's Bar
Calle Vallaresso; tel: 041-528 5777; all day, till late; vaporetto: San Marco/Vallaresso; map p. 137 E3
Go there for the atmosphere, the legendary Bellini cocktails and some celebrity spotting in surprisingly low-key surroundings. Also has an extremely good (and notoriously pricey) menu.

Martini Scala
Campo San Fantin, tel: 041-522 4121; Wed–Mon; daily 10am–3pm, closed July and Aug.; vaporetto: S. M. del Giglio; map p.137 E3
This is a slightly lacklustre piano bar and supper club but worth knowing about because it stays open very late.

CASTELLO
Most upmarket nightlife seems to revolve around the international hotels on the Riva degli Schiavoni. Nightlife is more Venetian in the authentic wine-bars behind San Zaccaria.

Enoteca Mascareta
Calle Lunga Santa Matria Formosa; tel: 041-523 0744; daily 7pm–2am; vaporetto: S. Zaccaria Jolanda/Danieli; map p.138 C3
Low-key temple to good

Above: cocktail hour at a busy *bacaro*.

wine and the lost art of conversation.

Inishark
Calle del Mondo Novo; tel: 041-523 5300; Tues–Sun 6pm–1.30am; vaporetto: Rialto; map p.138 B3
Fake but fun, this is the place for Guinness, bar snacks, Celtic music and live sport on TV.

DORSODURO
Campo Santa Margherita is the centre of Venice's nightlife, and is awash with buzzing, youth-oriented bars. The following are all well-established venues, but a number of new ones are opening up, now that the neighbourhood has gained a reputation for late-night entertainment.

Bistro ai do Draghi
Campo Santa Margherita; tel: 041 528 9731; daily 8–11pm (later in summer); vaporetto: Ca'Rezzonico; map p.136 B3
Watch the world go by over an *ombra* or spritz at this music bar at the northern end

of the square. You can also enjoy snacks such as *caparossoli* (clams) or excellent *tramezzini* (sandwiches).

Imagina
Ria Terra Canal; tel: 041-241 0625; open 8am–2am, closed Sun; vaporetto: Ca'Rezzonico; map p.136 B3
An arty, designer bar that comes into its own at night, with an eclectic programme of music and a selection of late-night snacks. Good cocktails draw a bohemian crowd but it becomes more youth-oriented as the night wears on.
SEE ALSO NIGHTLIFE, P.34–5

Margaret DuChamp
Campo Santa Margherita; tel: 041-528 6255; open 9pm–2am; vaporetto: ca'Rezzonico; map p.136 B3
A cool clientele is drawn to the equally cool atmosphere. Prices are reasonable and the service is friendly.

Orange
Campo Santa Margherita; tel: 041-523 4740; closed Sun; vaporetto: Ca'Rezzonico;

map p.136 B3
This contemporary lounge bar, with an in-house DJ is one of the current hotspots.

Piccolo Mondo 'El Suk'
Calle Contarini-Corfu; tel: 041-520 0371; entrance charge; open late; vaporetto: Accademia; map p.136 C2
Inconspicuous disco tucked away in an alley near the Accademia bridge. Mainly house music.

Suzie Café
Campo San Basilio; tel: 041 522 7502; closed Sunday; vaporetto: San Basilio; map p.136 B2
Suzie's stages live music in summer, from rock to reggae and blues.

CANNAREGIO
This northern part of town is generally quiet by night but the Fondamenta della Misericordia has a cluster of canalside nightspots with a good atmosphere and fairly decent food.

Casanova
Lista di Spagna; tel: 041-275 0199; entrance charge; bar and restaurant from 6pm, disco 10pm–4am; vaporetto: Fer Bar Roma; map p.134 B2
Unremarkable disco by the railway station with a range of music from rock to house.

Paradiso Perduto
Fondamenta della Misericordia; tel: 041-720 581; open 7pm–1am (Sat till 2am); vaporetto: S.Marcuola; map p.135 D3
This bustling bar attracts a trendy, arty young crowd, representative of the 'new' Venetian nightlife. There is

For a late-night ice cream, coffee or liqueur go to **Paolin** on Campo Santo Stefano (San Marco), one of the few *gelatarie* open very late (until midnight in summer). Try the pistachio or lemon ice-cream.

always background or live music (jazz, folk or ethnic), accompanied by typical hearty Venetian fare.

SAN POLO AND SANTA CROCE

Bacaro Jazz

Rialto Bridge (San Marco side, facing Fondaco dei Tedeschi); tel: 041-528 5249; closed Wed; vaporetto: Rialto; map p.137 E4

Restaurant and wine bar where you can enjoy cocktails, international and local cuisine and jazz DVDs and CDs. Occasional live music. Meals are served from 4pm–3am; happy hour is 4–7pm.

Osteria Ruga Rialto

Ruga Rialto; tel: 041-521 1243; open daily 11am-3pm, 6pm-midnight; p137 E4

A spacious and lively osteria offering live jazz, blues and reggae, as well as a range of inexpensive meals and/or drinks in a charming rustic setting.

The Lido has a wide range of atmospheric clubs that are fun in summer. You may also find yourself rubbing shoulders with the glitzy set, especially during the film festival.

Pachuka

San Nicolò beach; daily until 4am in season; vaporetto: S. Nicolò; map p.26

This is a popular beach bar, restaurant and disco-bar with live music and DJ-led events staged on the beach.

The Casino

Palazzo Vendramin-Calergi, Grand Canal; tel: 041-529 7111; www.casinovenezia.it; daily 11am–3am for slot machines, 3pm–3am for traditional gambling; vaporetto: San Marcuola; map p.135 C2

The casino is worth a visit as it allows you to appreciate the splendour of this Renaissance palazzo; one of the finest on the Grand Canal.

The casino focuses more on 'classic' table games – roulette, chemin de fer, baccarat, blackjack – rather than on American-style slot machines, but the latter are there too, and can be played earlier in the day (from 11am).

Smart clothes are required here, with jacket and tie compulsory for men; remember to take your passport or another official form of identification along with you.

Theatre

Teatro Al'Avogaria

Calle de l'Avogaria, Dorsoduro;

Above: tourists boarding for a gondola night-ride.

tel: 041-520 61 30; vaporetto: S. Basilio; map p.136 B2

Performs Commedia dell'Arte works. These originated in the 16th century as a form of comic theatre and produced memorable characters such as Harlequin, Pantalone and Pulcinella. The latter turned into Mr Punch in English Punch and Judy shows. The main interest of these works for visitors today may be that they were the inspiration behind many of the most distinctive carnival costumes and masks.

Teatro Goldoni

Calle Goldoni, San Marco 4650; tel: 041-240 2011; www.teatro-goldoni.it; vaporetto: S. Marco Vallaresso; map p.138 B2

Stages plays by the 18th-century Venetian dramatist Carlo Goldoni, as well as other dramatic works. It is also a music venue.

Other Options

For further information and recommendations for evening entertainment: SEE ALSO FILM, P.52; MUSIC, P.84, RESTAURANTS, P.106

Left: the Rialto Bridge at night.

Painting

Venice's status as a great trading empire exposed it to new artistic influences, first from Byzantium and later from Flanders and the Italian schools of Padua, Mantua, Ferrara and Florence. But Venetian art was less formulaic than other schools, with the greatest painters free to form their own inimitable personal styles. Light, colour, texture and space were the touchstones of Venetian art, in contrast to line and form in rival Florence. Tracking down the works of Venice's most prolific painters will take you all over the city from Cannaregio to San Polo, Dorsoduro to the Doge's Palace.

The Bellini Family

Jacopo Bellini and his two sons, Gentile and Giovanni, played a dominant role in Venetian art from 1400–1470. Venice was slow to absorb Renaissance values, but largely thanks to Giovanni Bellini (c. 1430–1516), evolved its own expressive style. Influenced by his Paduan brother-in-law, Mantegna, he had an understanding of perspective, and was one of the first Venetian artists to include landscapes in the background of his paintings. He revitalised Venetian painting, infusing his art with light, which was literally seen as a medium of grace. His brother, Gentile (1429–1507), rose to be official State painter, but in later years Giovanni succeeded him in this role.

Vittorio Carpaccio (c. 1465–1523/6)

Unlike Giovanni Bellini, Carpaccio was more interested in everyday life than in mood. He was the most Venetian of painters, although compared to Giorgione and Titian he was not innovative,

Above: detail from Titian's Pesaro Altarpiece in the Frari.

and his paintings have a static quality beneath the surface bustle. Yet the influence of Flemish art is apparent in his miniaturist precision, the details of faces and scenery. His finest works can be seen in the **Scuola di San Giorgio degli Schiavoni** and the **Accademia**.

SEE ALSO MUSEUMS AND GALLERIES, P.81; SCUOLE P.119

Giorgione (c. 1478–1510)

Giorgione has been called 'the first modern artist' thanks to the subjectivity of his vision. There are tantalisingly few of his paintings in existence. In

Venice, he is noted for two works in the **Accademia**: La Vecchia is both a realistic portrait of an elderly woman and a meditation on old age. Poignantly, Giorgione died in his early 30s, probably of the plague. The famous Tempest is a poetic and puzzling work that conveys a sense of enchantment disturbed by a mysterious inner tension.

SEE ALSO MUSEUMS AND GALLERIES, P.81

Titian (1487–1586)

Titian was the polished master of the Venetian High-Renaissance style. His range remains unsurpassed in Western art, encompassing portraits, paintings, mythological 'poesy', allegories and altarpieces. Titian's greatest paintings in Venice are in the **Frari**, where the revolutionary nature of The Assumption

> Few of Titian's works remain in Venice, thanks in part to Napoleon commandeering the artist's canvases as the spoils of war: Venice's loss was the Louvre's gain.

Left: Bellini's *Pietà* in the Accademia.

church of **San Sebastiano** (where appropriately he is buried) shows Veronese in all his glory.
SEE ALSO CHURCHES, P.44; PALAZZI P.93

Canaletto (1697–1768)

Antonio Canal, known as Canaletto, was greatly admired for his limpid land-scapes and almost photo-graphic observations. In Venice he worked from nature, which was unusual for the period, creating detailed views that influenced generations of painters. Grand-tourists who flocked to Venice at the time became collectors of Canaletto's paintings, and very little of his work remains in the city itself.

Tiepolo (1696–1770)

Giambattista Tiepolo is cele-brated for his sublime artifice, heroic style and a virtuosity reminiscent of the Old Masters. He was taken under the wing of the Venetian aristocracy and was commis-sioned to fresco some of the city's finest palaces. Tiepolo's mastery of the medium and flamboyant style took him from Venice to the royal courts of Europe.

vies with the secular opu-lence of the Pesaro altar-piece. The **Accademia** possesses a handful of Titian's works, notably his powerful *Pietà,* which he had intended for his own tomb.
SEE ALSO CHURCHES, P.43; MUSEUMS AND GALLERIES, P.81

Tintoretto (1518–94)

Tintoretto acquired his nick-name 'the little dyer' after his father's trade as a silk-dyer. The artist boldly stated that his aim was to 'reconcile the drawing of Michelangelo with the colours of Titian'. Michelangelo's influence is clear in Tintoretto's virile com-positions and battles with per-spective and bold fore-shortening; his debt to Titian is obvious in his love of colour and mood; but these are from a bold, less subtle palette, dominated by virtuoso *chiaroscuro* effects. Tintoretto brought a new passion and religious fervour to Venetian painting. His greatest works of art are the series of paintings which adorn the city's **Scuola Grande di San Rocco.**
SEE ALSO SCUOLE, P.120

Veronese (1528–88)

Veronese was nicknamed after his native city, Verona, but his concerns were utterly Venet-ian. As a colourist, he was the true successor to Bellini, while in his striving for splendour and decorative detail, his works echoed the Byzantine style. As a society painter, he portrayed the patrician ideal; a civilised life of leisure, a parade of sumptuous fabrics and Palladian decoration. Veronese captured the taste of the times, and was chosen to work on the decoration of the **Doge's Palace.** The resplen-dent cycle of paintings in the

Below: Tiepolo's flights of fantasy in the Carmini.

Palazzi

The palace (*palazzo*) is the classic unit of Venetian architecture, a form influenced by the Roman country-villa and by Byzantine buildings in Ravenna and Constantinople. The city succumbed to the spell of the East – from marble to mosaics, the eastern colonies provided precious materials to transform the inhospitable lagoon islands into an imperial capital. The Byzantine spirit was poured into a Gothic mould; only reluctantly, and fairly late, was Venice lured into the Renaissance. Characterised by colour, decoration and eclecticism, the result is a synthesis of styles known simply as Venetian.

Shapes and Styles

Although many of the frescoed façades of Venetian *palazzi* have not survived the ravages of time and humidity, some along the Grand Canal have been sympathetically recreated. Yet the vernacular Venetian style is a hybrid. A typical cluster of buildings may show influences from East and West, sporting Moorish windows, a Gothic structure, Veneto-Byzantine decoration and Renaissance or Baroque flourishes. Plaques and roundels create *chiaroscuro* effects and offset the flatness of the façade; and the vivid marble reflects the local love of colour.

Thanks to inheritance laws, financial vicissitudes and the extinction of the old ducal families, few families inhabit their ancestral homes. Yet impoverished aristocrats may languish in part of a palace or live in one which, while not bearing their name, has been in the family for

Left: looking down the Scala d'Oro – the golden staircase – of the Palazzo Ducale.

centuries. Other palaces belong to residents who relish the soft opulence of their second homes.

Many palaces have become hotels or showcases for Venetian glass and textile manufacturers. Some are now the repositories of great collections of art.

Consequently, the following list includes buildings that have been mentioned in the section on Museums and Galleries *(see page 74)* but here we concentrate on the buildings themselves rather than on the contents. Most of the palaces, however, must be admired from the outside as they are not open to the public; opening times are given for those that are accessible.

San Marco

Palazzo Contarini del Bovolo

Corte Contarini del Bovolo; Apr–Oct: 10am–6pm, Nov–Mar: Sat and Sun 10am–4pm; entrance charge; vaporetto: Sant'Angelo or Rialto; map p.138 A2 This late-Gothic palace is celebrated for its romantic arcaded staircase. Bovolo,

Left: The Palazzo Ducale's façade, a Venetian Gothic masterpiece.

ian Gothic masterpiece, including the porticoes and ceremonial balcony overlooking the quays. The **Sala del Maggior Consiglio** was rebuilt in 1340, transforming this water-front wing. The **Porta della Carta**, the main ceremonial gateway, is a triumph of flamboyant Gothic style. **The Scala dei Giganti**, the Giants' Stairway, was built in 1486 to provide access to the loggia on the first floor.

Inside, the **Scala d'Oro**, designed by Sansovino in 1555, is a ceremonial staircase linking the *piano nobile* with the ostentatious rooms on the upper floors, such as the **Sala del Collegio**, where ambassadors were received. The **Collegiate Rooms** are lavishly decorated with mythological scenes by Tintoretto and Veronese. The **Sala del Consiglio dei Dieci** was the chamber where the feared Council of Ten tried crimes against the state. The **Sala del Maggior Consiglio**, the Grand Council Chamber, is a highlight, a grandiose affair studded with coffered

The best way to see the Doge's Palace without the crowds is to book the 'Secret Itinerary', which explores behind the scenes (in English, French and Italian; tel: 041-271 5911).

meaning snail-shell in Venetian dialect, well describes the delightful spiral staircase, which is linked to loggias of brick and smooth white stone. You can climb the staircase, but the interior of the palace cannot be visited.

Palazzo Ducale

Piazzetta; Apr–Oct: daily 9am–7pm; Nov–Mar: 9am–5pm; entrance charge; vaporetto: San Zaccaria; map p.138 C2

The **Doge's Palace** is the greatest palazzo of them all. It was the seat of the Venetian government from the 9th century until the fall of the Republic in 1797. The palace was a symbol of political stability and independence, as well as a testament to Venetian supremacy and a glorious showcase of art, sculpture and craftsmanship. Yet there was also a shadowy side to

the palace, a secretive machine staffed by State inquisitors, spies and torturers-in-residence.

Although often considered the symbol of Gothic Venice, the palace's distinctive façades were inspired by the Veneto-Byzantine succession of porticoes and loggias. The palace has two of the finest Gothic façades in existence, a vision of rosy Verona marble supported by Istrian stone arcades. The harmonious waterfront façade is a Venet-

Below: the open arcades of the Palazzo Ducale.

Palazzo Ducale

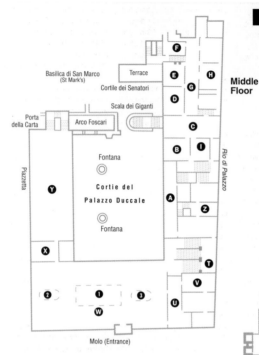

Basilica di San Marco
(St Mark's)

Terrace

Cortile dei Senatori

Middle Floor

Scala dei Giganti

Porta della Carta

Arco Foscari

Fontana

Cortie del Palazzo Duccale

Piazzetta

Fontana

Rio di Palazzo

Molo (Entrance)

Top Floor

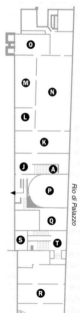

Rio di Palazzo

- **A** Scala d'Oro (Golden Staircase)
- **B** Sala degli Scarlatti (Robing Room)
- **C** Sala dello Scudo (Shield Room)
- **D** Sala Grimani
- **E** Sala Erizzo
- **F** Sala degli Stucchi (Stucco Room)
- **G** Sala dei Filosofi (Philosophers' Room)
- **H** Ducale's residence
- **I** Sala degli Scudieri (Palace Guardroom)
- **J** Atrio Quadrato
- **K** Sala delle Quattro Porte (Room of Four Doors)
- **L** Sala dell' Anticollegio
- **M** Sala del Collegio
- **N** Sala del Senato
- **O** Chiesetta (The Ducale's private chapel)
- **P** Sala del Consiglio dei Dieci (Seat of the Council of Ten)
- **Q** Sala della Bussola (Compass Room)
- **R** Armeria (Armoury)
- **S** Sala degli Inquisitori (Inquisition Room)
- **T** Scala dei Censori (Censors' Staircase)
- **U** Andito del Maggior Consiglio (Corridor of the Great Council)
- **V** Sala della Quarantia Civil Vecchia (Old Courtroom)
- **W** Sala del Maggior Consiglio (Hall of Great Council) with paintings by
  (**1**) Tintotretto (**2**) Palma Il Giovane (**3**) Veronese
- **X** Sala della Quarantia Civil Nuova (New Courtroom)
- **Y** Sala dello Scrutinio
- **Z** Sala della Quarantia Criminale

Buildings in Venice are supported on closely-packed piles of timber, which were driven into the solid *caranto* (compressed clay and sand) at the bottom of the lagoon.

ceilings, paintings and embossed surfaces.

Palazzo Fortuny

Campo San Beneto; vaporetto: Sant' Angelo; map p.138 A2

A late-Gothic palace, built for the Pesaro family at the end of the 15th century. It was acquired by Mariano Fortuny – photographer, painter and textile designer – at the beginning of the 20th century. He lived there until his death in 1949, and his widow sold it to the Venice city council some seven years later. The palace is undergoing restoration but some rooms are open for Fortuny-related temporary exhibitions.

Canale Grande

The following list details palaces running along the right bank of the Grand Canal, starting from San Marco, and returning along the opposite bank.

RIGHT BANK

Palazzo Giustinian

Vaporetto: San Marco-Vallaresso; map p.138 B1

The Giustiniani were an illustrious dynasty tracing their origins to the Roman Empire. Legend has it that in the 12th century, the line was threatened with extinction, and the sole remaining heir was persuaded to leave his monastery for marriage to the doge's daughter. After saving the line by siring 12 offspring, he returned to a life of celibate seclusion. His

sacrifice was a success: the Venetian branch only died out in 1962. In the 19th century, the palace was a hotel where Proust, Turner and Verdi stayed. A newly wed George Eliot stayed here with her unstable husband until he jumped from their window into the canal. The palace is now the headquarters of the Venice Biennale.

Palazzo Contarini-Fasan

Vaporetto: San Marco-Vallaresso; map p.138 A1

This model of late-Gothic design in miniature has subtle carved cable-moulding on the façade. It is nicknamed 'Desdemona's House', since it supposedly inspired the setting for Desdemona's home in Shakespeare's *Othello*.

Palazzo Pisani-Gritti

Vaporetto: Santa Maria del Giglio; map p.138 A1

Also known as the Gritti Palace, this is one of Venice's most sumptuous hotels, replete with Murano glass chandeliers and 16th-century damask furnishings. It is linked to writers as diverse as Hemingway and Graham Greene. Ruskin and his wife stayed here rather than being tempted by the decadent

notion of 'hiring a house or palace – it sounds too Byronish or Shelleyish.'

Palazzo Contarini-Polignac

Vaporetto: Santa Maria del Giglio; map p.138 A1

This was one of the first Renaissance palaces in Venice. It was, in fact, a Gothic building, to which a Renaissance façade decorated with marble roundels was added. The Princesse de Polignac ran a sophisticated 19th-century salon here, and the palace remains in the same family.

Ca' Grande

Free guided tours by appointment, for information and booking tel: 041-296 0726; vaporetto: Santa Maria del Giglio; map p.138 A1

Ca' Corner della Ca' Grande, to give it its full name, is one of the greatest of Venetian palaces, both in terms of importance and sheer size. Built by Sansovino for Jacopo Corner, a nephew of the queen of Cyprus, the palace is the first confident High Renaissance building in Venice. The Corner dynasty had deep links with Venice and owned numerous palaces in the city. The last of the line sold this one to the Austrian

Right: entrance to the Palazzo Fortuny.

95

Above: the filigree façade of the Ca' d'Oro.

administration in 1812, and the palace is now the seat of the Prefecture, the provincial government.

Palazzo Barbaro
Vaporetto: Accademia; map p.137 D2

This is a Gothic gem, built for the Barbaro family, who made their fortune in the salt trade. In the late 19th century, Monet, Browning and Henry James were all guests of the Bostonian Curtis family who then owned part of the building. James wrote *The Aspern Papers* here, and set *The Wings of a Dove* in his rooms. The film of the same name was later filmed in the palace.

Palazzo Cavalli-Franchetti
Vaporetto: Accademia; map p.137 D2

A grandiose late-Gothic palace, begun around 1565.

For three centuries it was shared by various illustrious Venetian families, and in the mid-19th century it was modernised by Archduke Frederick of Austria. Since 1999 it has been the property of the Venetian Institute of Science, Letters and Art, who turned it into a cultural and conference centre. The palace has richly ornamented window-frames and an appealing garden.

Palazzo Falier
Vaporetto: San Samuele or Accademia; map p.137 D2

An early-Gothic palace, smaller than many on the canal, and distinguished by twin Venetian loggias (*liaghi*) facing the canal. This was supposedly the home of the infamous Doge Marin Falier, beheaded for treason in 1355.

Palazzo Grassi
Daily 10am–7pm, last admission 6pm; entrance charge; vaporetto: San Samuele; map p.137 D3

Beside the San Samuele landing stage looms this formidable palace, which has recently re-opened as a major exhibition centre after a long period of closure. This imposing patrician palace is a model of Neoclassical restraint. Although it was based on plans by Longhena there is no trace of Baroque exuberance; Massari completed the building in the 18th century, making it the last palace to be constructed before the fall of the Republic. In 2005 it was bought by a French business magnate, François Pinault, and renovated by Japanese architect Tadao Ando. Original materials, marble and stucco, have been retained and reused where possible.

Ca' Mocenigo
Vaporetto: Sant' Angelo; map p.137 C3

This cluster of palaces belonged to the influential Mocenigo family, who produced seven doges. Byron stayed here while writing his mock-heroic poem Don Juan (1819–24) and had an affair with the baker's wife, a woman 'wild as a witch and fierce as a demon'.

Palazzo Corner-Spinelli
Vaporetto: Sant' Angelo; map p.137 D3

This is the prototype of a Renaissance palace. Designed by Coducci, it has

> Most of the great palazzi line the Grand Canal. Purchase a day pass and trail up and down to your heart's content, stopping as the fancy takes you (vaporetto lines 1 and 82 cover the route).

a rusticated ground floor as well as his trademark windows, two bold round-arched lights framed by a single round arch. Like Ca' Grande, the palace was owned by the Corner family, the royal Cypriot dynasty. The ownership passed to the Spinelli, important dealers in gold and silks, and still serves as the showrooms of noted Venetian textile merchants today.

Palazzo Loredan

Vaporetto: Rialto; map p.138 A3

Graced with the original capitals, arches and plaques, Loredan is one of the finest Veneto-Byzantine palaces in Venice, rivalled only by its neighbour, Palazzo Farsetti. The pair are occupied by the city council and the mayor.

Ca' da Mosto

Vaporetto: Ca' d'Oro; map p.138 B4

This 13th-century palace is a fine, but crumbling example of Veneto-Byzantine architecture, and the birthplace in 1432 of Alvise da Mosto, credited with discovering the Cape Verde Islands. From the 16th to the 18th century it

was the Leon Bianco Inn, Venice's leading hotel, whose guests included Emperor Joseph II and the painter J.M.W. Turner.

Ca' d'Oro

Mon 8.15am–2pm, Tues–Sun 8.15am–7.15pm; entrance charge; vaporetto: Ca' d'Oro; map p.138 A4

Generally regarded as the loveliest of the city's Gothic palaces, set beside the landing stage of the same name. Architecturally, this is a landmark building and a sumptuous version of a Venetian palace. On the façade, the friezes of interlaced foliage and mythological beasts were originally picked out in gold, leading to its popular name, the 'House of Gold'. The Veneto-Byzantine influence is clear in the design, from the oriental pinnacles to the ethereal tracery.

As well as the water-gate on the Grand Canal, the palace retains its original landgate in a brick courtyard. The palace was insensitively 'restored' in the mid-19th century, but Baron Franchetti, a later owner, returned it to its

Striped mooring posts feature prominently alongside palaces of the Grand Canal. The colours signify that they belong to a specific family and the posts may be topped with a family crest.

original glory, even tracking down the original staircases. Suffering from an incurable illness, the baron committed suicide in 1922, but not before bequeathing his beloved palace to the city. The courtyard contains the original Gothic well-head that Franchetti finally retrieved from a Parisian dealer. Although the interior is no longer recognisably Gothic, the coffered ceilings and fine marble floors make a splendid showcase for the medieval and Renaissance exhibits.

Palazzo Vendramin-Calergi

Vaporetto: San Marcuola; map p.135 C2

Vendramin-Calergi was built around 1500 by Coducci for the patrician Loredan dynasty. The Vendramin, scions of a banking and ducal

Below: exterior detail of the Ca' da Mosto.

Below: detail of a side door of the Ca' d'Oro.

family, then owned the palace until 1845, when it was sold to the French Bourbon Duchesse de Berry. Here she based her court in exile, a Versailles on the lagoon. Wagner rented the mezzanine wing from the family and, with his father-in-law Franz Liszt, gave a concert at La Fenice opera house. In 1883, Wagner suffered a stroke in his apartments and died in his wife's arms. The palace is a Classical masterpiece, built in familiar three-part design and faced with Istrian stone. It still possesses a spectacular interior, now home of the **city casino**, with coffered ceilings, chandeliers, marble fireplaces and Mannerist paintings, as well as a hall decorated with jasper columns from the Turkish ruins of Ephesus.

SEE ALSO NIGHTLIFE, P.89;

LEFT BANK

Ca' Pesaro

Tue–Sun 10am–5pm; entrance charge; vaporetto: San Stae; map p.135 D2

A stately Baroque pile, designed by Longhena. The well-restored Grand Canal façade offers a play of *chiaroscuro* effects created by recessed windows and sharply delineated cornices. The rusticated ground-floor façade is interrupted by a triple-arched water entrance leading to a theatrical inner courtyard lined by balconies, loggias and a portico, with a grand well-head in the centre. In 1899, Duchess Bevilacqua La Masa bequeathed the palace to the city. It is now home to the **Museum of Oriental Art** and the **Gallery of Modern Art**. Henry James said of the palace: 'I even have a timid kindness for the

A number of Venetian palaces have very similar names. They were often the seats of separate branches of one family, so their names bear witness to Venetian fortunes, feuds and intermarriages.

huge Pesaro, whose main reproach, more even than the coarseness of its forms, is its swaggering size'.

SEE ALSO MUSEUMS AND GALLERIES, P.76–7

Ca' Corner della Regina
Vaporetto: San Stae; map p.135 D1

The birthplace of Caterina Corner, Queen of Cyprus, who was the victim of a cynical Venetian plot to gain control of the island. In the 17th century, descendants of her family rebuilt the palace, which is now owned by the Biennale organisation.

Palazzo dei Camerlenghi
Vaporetto: Rialto; map p.137 E4

Now a courthouse, the palace was built in 1525 as the seat of the exchequer, with the ground floor used as a debtors' prison. Like many multifunctional Venetian buildings, it also served as a merchants' emporium and administrative centre.

Palazzo Grimani
Vaporetto: San Silvestro or San Tomà; map p.137 D4

Austere-looking Renaissance palace by Michele Sanmichele, now serving as the Court of Appeal.

Palazzo Pisani-Moretta
Vaporetto: San Tomà; map p.137 D3

Embellished with Gothic tracery, the Pisani-Moretta is reminiscent of the Doge's Palace. Curiously, the palace has two *piani nobili* or patrician floors instead of one. The palace is also exceptional in still belonging to descendants of the Pisani family.

Below: Ca' Pesaro.

Above: the ballroom of Ca' Rezzonico.

Palazzo Balbi
Vaporetto: San Tomà; map p.137 C2

Conspicuous for its pinnacles, this palace was the chosen site for Napoléon to watch the regatta of 1807, held in his honour.

Ca' Foscari
Vaporetto: Ca' Rezzonico or San Tomà; map p.137 C3

Built at the height of Venetian power, this is a monument to the ambition of Doge Foscari, who ruled from 1423 to 1457. Tommaso Mocenigo, a previous doge, distrusted him: 'he sweeps and soars more than a hawk or a falcon'. Foscari survived to pursue expansionist goals until a conspiracy caused his downfall, and he died in this palace, a broken man. It is one of the last Late Gothic structures in the city. The façade has fine tracery, and a frieze of putti bearing the Foscari arms. This Gothic stage-set witnessed countless pageants. During a state visit prior to being crowned, Henri III of France stayed here and was fêted by the Venetians.

The mosaic floor of his bedroom was remodelled to Veronese's designs; Titian painted his portrait and Palladio was commissioned to build a triumphal arch. Now the grandest part of Venice University, the palace has been tampered with but is being restored.

Palazzo Giustinian
Vaporetto: Ca' Rezzonico; map p.137 C3

Below: Ca' Foscari.

Not to be confused with the eponymous palace on the other side of the canal, this is one of 15 palaces owned by the Giustiniani clan. The Gothic showpiece is a double palace adorned with delicate tracery and linked by a water-gate. Wagner composed *Tristan und Isolde* (1857–59) here.

Ca' Rezzonico
Wed-Mon 10am–4pm; entrance charge; vaporetto: Ca' Rezzonico; map p.137 C2

The Rococo interior has been sumptuously restored in recent years, and now houses the **Museum of 18th-Century Venetian Life**. In keeping with Venetian style, the rooms are sparsely but lavishly furnished, with the mirrored wall-brackets, lacquered furniture and chinoiserie that characterised the period. A grand staircase leads to the *piano nobile*, the ceremonial first floor added by Massari. Here, the opulent setting makes a spectacular showcase for Tiepolo's trompe l'oeil ceil-

99

ings and Guardi's memorable genre scenes. The *sala da ballo*, or ballroom, is boldly restored, daringly frescoed and richly embellished with glittering chandeliers and period pieces, including ebony vase-stands borne by Moors.
SEE ALSO MUSEUMS AND GALLERIES, P.77

Palazzo Venier dei Leoni
Wed–Mon 10am–6pm; entrance charge; vaporetto: Salute or Accademia; map p.137 D1
This white, truncated structure is known as the Palazzo Nonfinito (Unfinished). Legend has it that the owners of the Ca' Grande on the opposite side of the canal forbade further building as it would block the view, but it is more likely that the project simply ran out of funds. Although now restricted to two storeys, the original structure was intended to rival the city's grandest. This 18th-century palace was built for one of the oldest Venetian dynasties, who produced three doges. The Veniers' lion nickname (dei Leoni) derives from the pet lion they kept chained in the courtyard. The building now houses the **Peggy Guggenheim Collection**.
SEE ALSO MUSEUMS AND GALLERIES, P78

Ca' Dario
Vaporetto: Salute; map p.137 D1
The gently listing Ca' Dario is one of the most delightful spots on the Grand Canal. Henry James adored this Gothic palace, then let to motley foreigners. However, five centuries of scandals, suicides and suspicious deaths have given it a reputation for being haunted. It belonged to Giovanni Dario, who negotiated peace with the Turks in 1479. Dario's daughter died of a broken heart after marrying into the patrician Barbaro family. Although the Dario family retained ownership until the 19th century, tragedy regularly struck its members, including a family massacre. Another purchaser, an Armenian diamond merchant, swiftly went bankrupt, while in the 1840s, aesthete Rawdon

> The great Venetian houses are usually known as *palazzi* (the plural of *palazzo*) but sometimes the word *Ca'* is used instead – *Ca'* simply being an abbreviation of casa, meaning house. This does not necessarily indicate they are less grand than palazzi.

Brown committed suicide in the drawing room. In 1936, French poet Henri de Régnier died shortly after moving in. During the 1970s the then owner, Kit Lambert, manager of The Who, was murdered over a drugs dispute. In 1979 the jinx struck Count delle Lanze, battered to death with a candlestick by his male lover. The most recent victim was industrialist Raul Gardini, who committed suicide in 1993 after being linked to corruption scandals. The palace is now to be used as exhibition space for the local Peggy Guggenheim Collection.
SEE ALSO MUSEUMS AND GALLERIES, P78

Palazzo Salviati
Vaporetto: Salute; map p.137 D1
Lying between Ca' Dario and Ca' Genovese, this 1920s palazzo is notable for its vivid mosaics in an ochre façade.

Castello

Palazzo Vitturi
Campo Santa Maria Formosa; vaporetto: Rialto or San Zaccaria; map p.138 C3
A 13th-century affair decorated with Gothic and Moorish motifs, this palace is now a smart hotel.

Palazzo Trevisan-Cappello
Rio di Canonica; vaporetto: San Zaccaria; map p.138 C3
A stately Renaissance palace studded with slender columns and ornamentation, this was the home of Bianca

Below: Venetian dramatist, Carlo Goldoni (1707–1793).

Above: cursed canalside palace, Ca' Dario.

Cappello, wife of Francesco de' Medici.

San Polo and Santa Croce

Casa Goldoni

Calle dei Nomboli, San Polo; Thur–Tue 10am–5pm (4pm winter); entrance charge; vaporetto: San Tomà; map p.137 C3

The birthplace of Carlo Goldoni, the 18th-century Venetian dramatist. Even if you are not interested in the writer, you can enjoy the attractive courtyard with a carved well-head and Gothic staircase.

Palazzo Mocenigo

Salizzada San Stae, Santa Croce; Tue–Sun 10am–5pm (4pm winter); entrance charge; vaporetto: San Stae; map p.135 C1

This palace-museum is linked to one of the greatest ducal families. The ancestral home was so well-preserved that, after Alvise Mocenigo bequeathed it to the city in 1954, it became a fitting showcase of gracious 18th-century living, from the lavishly decorated ballroom to the frescoed bedchamber. The palatial mansion remains

an airless time capsule, defined by its Murano chandeliers, gilded furnishings and Rococo frescos. This makes a perfect setting for a display of Venetian period costumes, as well as for a family-portrait gallery worthy of a dynasty that produced seven doges.

Cannaregio

Palazzo Labia

Campo San Geremia; closed for restoration; vaporetto: Guglie; map p.134 B2

This is a splendid neoclassical palace on the Cannaregio canal. The former owners, the wealthy Labia family from Catalonia, employed some of the most famous painters of the time to decorate it: Tiepolo produced some superb frescoes for the ballroom. The Labia family were renowned for their extravagance: once, after a riotous banquet, the gold plates were hurled into the canal as the host cried out: 'Le abbia o non le abbia sarò sempre Labia!' ('Whether I have them or not, I'll always be a Labia!') The occasion for this extravagant pun (which doesn't work so well in English) had been carefully contrived, with precautionary nets placed in the water to catch the precious heirlooms.

Dorsoduro

Palazzo Cini

Calle San Vio; vaporetto: Accademia; map p.137 D1

The former residence of industrialist Count Vittorio Cini (1884–1977) now houses his splendid art collection, including works by Botticelli, Filippo Lippi and Giunta Pisano.

Palazzo Zenobio

Rio Santa Margherita; vaporetto: Ca' Rezzonico; map p.136 B2

Although originally Gothic, this palace was remodelled in

the 17th century and given a long, monotonous façade, softened by Italianate gardens at the back. It has been an Armenian college since 1850. Although not officially open to the public you can sometimes gain access to the sumptuous ballroom, adorned by a minstrels' gallery, gold-and-white stuccowork and trompe l'oeil effects.

Murano

Palazzo da Mula

Fondamenta da Mula; vaporetto: Da Mula; map p.24

A glassworks in the splendid setting of a Gothic palace and Byzantine walled-garden.

Palazzo Trevisan

Fondamenta Andrea Navagero; vaporetto: Museo; map p.138 C3

Facing the Museo del Vetro, this 16th-century building (the third of the Venetian Trevisan palaces) has an interior frescoed by Veronese. The façade was once also decorated with frescoes but they have not survived.

Below: faded grandeur: a Cannaregio palace façade.

101

Pampering

The very name, Venice, suggests indulgence. It may be the image conjured from a thousand pictures of dreamy gondola rides and lights sparkling on water, or the fact that it is one of the top choices for honeymoons and St Valentine's Day breaks. Or perhaps it is because a city that has inspired so many writers and artists automatically gains a reputation for leisure and pleasure; and it is one that Venice does its best to live up to. Opportunities to indulge abound: stay in a lavish hotel on the Grand Canal, enjoy a candlelit dinner with a watery view, glide across the lagoon in a private launch – but be prepared to foot a very big bill.

Wellness Centres

A number of the better hotels have opened 'wellness centres' in recent years; places where you can do nothing but be pampered. One is the Palace Bonvecchiati, between Piazza San Marco and the Rialto (Calle dei Fabbri, tel: 041-296 3111; www.palace bonvecchiati.it) a delightful boutique hotel whose chic bedrooms are pretty indulgent, too.

Another is the swish Hotel Cipriani (Giudecca 10; tel: 041-240 8016; www.hotelcipriani.it) whose Casanova Beauty and Wellness Center is named after the legendary lover who once held clandestine trysts in the gardens of the hotel. Treatment rooms, offering every kind of massage imaginable, open on to private terraces with splashing fountains, and the 'fitness room' has views over the gardens.

A Night of Luxury

If you really want to be indulged and pampered it doesn't come cheap. If you've decided that money is no object, then a night in the Hemingway Suite at the Gritti Palace (Campo Santa Maria del Giglio; tel: 041-794 611; www.starwood.com/grittipalace) is the height of luxury. This 15th-century palace will cosset you with damask furnishings and glowing chandeliers,

Left: travel in style on a water launch or taxi.

Start as you mean to go on: splash out on a water taxi from the airport to San Marco. It costs around 90 euros but it's a magical way to see Venice for the first time and will make you feel like a star.

Left: the Casanova Beauty and Wellness Centre, at the Hotel Cipriani.

the night. Two other restaurants, both near San Marco, vie for the title of 'most romantic'. One is De Pisis (Hotel Bauer, Campo San Moisè; tel: 041-520 7022) where the views from the waterside terrace are matched by the excellence of the food. Try the 'tasting menu' if you want a real treat.

Alternatively, there is the Antico Martini (Campo San Fantini, San Marco; tel: 041-522 4121), a classic restaurant with a piano bar and a seductive setting among 18th-century paintings, pink damask napery, candlelight and gleaming crystal.

while reminding you that Greta Garbo was once a guest. And it's reputed to have the best Grand Canal terrace in town.

Alternatively, you could take one of the lagoon villa rooms in the Grand Hotel dei Dogi (Fondamenta Madonna dell'Orto; tel: 041-220 8111; www.boscolohotels.it). Set in the north of the city on the edge of the lagoon, this hotel has the largest and loveliest garden in Venice and carries an air of total peace and calm.

Drinking it In

You can't help but feel pampered as deferential waiters bring you Prosecco on silver salvers at the Caffè Florian in Piazza San Marco. A quite different but delightful experience is to be had at Linea d'Ombra (Ponte dell'Umiltà, Zattere; tel: 041-241 1881) in Dorsoduro. A drink (or meal) on the floating pontoon on a summer evening, with views across the water to Il Redentore church, is a delight.

Indulgent Dinners

If you want to feel really pampered, how about getting a private launch from San Marco to the island of San Clemente, where the San Clemente Hotel's Ca' dei Frati restaurant (tel: 041-244 5001), in a former monastery, is an enchanting setting for a meal, with views back across to St Mark's. If you don't want to leave, you could always book a room and stay

If you enjoy being cosseted and feeling special, forget about airlines and queues for check-in and travel to Venice by train on the **Orient Express** (tel: 0845-077 2222; www.orient-express.com). It's a travel experience like no other, with the style and glamour (and expense) of a bygone era.

Right: the Venice Simplon-Orient Express.

Parks and Gardens

The city has plenty of leafy squares but, with space so limited, there is a paucity of public parks and gardens. The loveliest of the green spaces tend to lie behind the high walls of private palazzi or the hard-to-access monastery precincts. The only notable public gardens of the city are the Giardini Pubblici in eastern Castello. However, if the streets of the centre become claustrophobic you can always hop on a ferry to the outlying islands for a nature ramble or an eco-tour of the lagoon.

Giardini Pubblici/ Biennale

Vaporetto: Giardini; map p.102 B2
The green lung of the city, the public gardens follow the waterfront all the way from the Arsenale vaporetto stop to Sant'Elena. Although rather unkempt, the gardens have some fine trees, and along the waterfront there are shady benches where you can relax and enjoy lovely lagoon views.

The stretch at the western end is home to the Venetian Biennale, with garden-lined paths leading to designer pavilions. About 40 countries are represented in these permanent pavilions, with space set aside for international exhibitions. The pastoral nature of the site makes a pleasing contrast to the slick modernism of the exhibits. A number of pavilions have been built by famous architects, notably Josef Hoffman's Austrian pavilion (1934), the Venetian architect Carlo Scarpa's Venezuelan pavilion (1954) and Alvar Aalto's Finnish creation (1956). The best spots are taken by the old-

Above: having a siesta in the Giardini Pubblici.

world powers. According to art critic Waldemar Januszczak, distortions of national rivalries are alive and well: 'the British pavilion stares across at the German'; and while the British space is vaguely Palladian and looks as though it would do a nice line in teas, the German building is 'one of the few bits of full-blown Nazi architecture to survive outside Germany'. One of the more recent additions is James

Stirling's Book Pavilion (1994), facing the vast Italian pavilion. Inspired by naval design and intended to recall the neighbouring Arsenale, this spacious glass-and-copper structure resembles an overgrown vaporetto.

From the Giardini pavilions you can follow the shoreline east through the Parco delle Rimembranze.

San Michele

Enclosed within high walls the cemetery island of San Michele lies north of the historic centre, just across the water from the Fondamente Nuove. It was here that Napoleon decreed the dead should be despatched across the water, away from the crowded city graves. The Austrians used the former monastery as a political prison, but the island is now tended by Franciscans.

The cemetery occupies most of the island. Famous foreigners are allowed to rest in peace, but more modest souls tend to be evicted after 10 years and taken to the mainland.

Left: the formal garden of a Venetian palazzo.

Around Piazza San Marco the only place you can picnic without incurring a fine is the Giardinetti Reali (Royal Gardens), beside the Venice Pavilion (tourist office).

Nature Excursions

For a different side of Venice try a nature ramble on the lesser-known lagoon islands. You can visit the market gardens on the island of Sant'Erasmo, fish farms in the lagoon, or visit the peaceful monastery islands of San Lazzaro degli Armeni (daily 3.25– 5.25pm, Line 20 from San Zaccaria) with a church and monastery set in lovely gardens, and San Francesco del Deserto (Tuesday to Sunday 9–11am, 3–5pm) which can only be accessed by hiring a boat from Burano.

For information on nature tours of the lagoon contact Limosa who run Natura Venezia (tel: 041-932003 www.natura-venezia.it). These lagoon tours are aimed at increasing the ecological awareness of visitors and Venetians alike.

The rambling cemetery is lined by gardens stacked with simple memorials or domed family mausoleums awaiting further members. Here lie the tombs of several ducal families, obscure diplomats, and the victims of malaria or the plague.

The grounds are studded with grotesque statuary, encompassing the monumental and the municipal, the cute and the kitsch. The most famous personalities are foreign. In the eastern corner is the Protestant *(Evangelisti)* section, containing the grave of American poet, **Ezra Pound** (1885–1972). Untended and overgrown, this is also the last resting place of obscure Swiss, German and British seamen.

In the *Greci* or Orthodox section lie the tombs of the composer **Igor Stravinsky** (1882–1971) and the ballet impresario **Sergei Diaghilev** (1872–1929), along with the tombs of some long-forgotten Russian and Greek aristocrats.

Below: Stravinsky's grave.

Below: San Michele cemetery.

Restaurants

Venetian restaurants range in style from cool, 18th-century elegance – especially in San Marco and Castello – to rustic gentility. Yet individualistic inns abound, tucked under pergolas or spilling onto terraces and courtyards. More upmarket places are termed *ristoranti*, but may be called *osterie* (inns) if they focus on homely food in an intimate or rustic setting. *Bacari* are traditional wine bars which also serve food; a Venetian version of tapas, known as *cichetti*. Where no closing times are given, restaurants are open daily for lunch and dinner. Reservations are required for the grander restaurants.

Piazza San Marco

Caffè Quadri
Procuratie Vecchie, Piazza San Marco; tel: 041-522 2105; closed Mon in winter; €€€; vaporetto: San Marco Giardinetti; map p.138 B2
In addition to the famous bar, this is the only proper restaurant on the piazza, serving Venetian dishes as well as creative twists on classic Italian cuisine. The seafood grill and risotto are recommended. Booking essential.
SEE ALSO BARS AND CAFÉS P.30

Above: interior of the atmospheric bistro-cum-wine bar, Le Bistrot de Venise.

Sestiere San Marco

Acqua Pazza
Campo Sant'Angelo; tel: 041-277 0688; closed Mon; €€€; vaporetto: S. Angelo; map p.137 D3
This lively pizzeria serves authentic Neapolitan pizzas and seafood. Bruschetta antipasti and a post-coffee limoncello are on the house.

Prices for an average three course meal with wine:	
€	under €30
€€	€30–€55
€€€	over €50

Antico Martini
Campo San Fantin; tel: 041-522 4121; €€€; vaporetto: S. M. Del Giglio; map p.137 E3
This classic restaurant, with piano bar and late opening hours, is a Venetian institution. The menu includes seafood risotto, *granseola* (spider crab) and *fegato alla veneziana* (liver on a bed of onions). Booking essential.

Le Bistrot de Venise
Calle dei Fabbri; tel: 041-523 6651; €€ (set menu) and €€€ (à la carte); vaporetto: San Marco Giardinetti; map p.138 B2;
Set behind St Mark's, this romantic wine-bar and bistro is a touch touristy, but redeemed by the canalside terrace, fine wines and seafood staples such as lobster and scampi.

Canova
Hotel Luna Baglioni, Calle Larga dell'Ascensione; tel: 041-528 9840; €€€; vaporetto: San Marco Vallaresso; map p.138 B1
This historic hotel's elegant restaurant has a menu that embraces international fare and Venetian staples, all prepared with the freshest ingredients; has memorable desserts.

Left: canalside terrace of Le Bistrot de Venise.

light, with service and food to match, and views from the terrace. Currently considered the best hotel restaurant in Venice: classic Italian cuisine with creative touches. Booking essential.

Trattoria Da Fiore
Calle delle Botteghe, off Campo Santo Stefano; tel: 041-523 5310; closed Tue; €€; vaporetto: Academia; map p.137 D3
Not to be confused with the pricy Da Fiore *(see p.112)*, this rustic but cosy trattoria is divided into a *bacaro* for wine and bar snacks *(cichetti)*, and a dining room that serves a full menu at higher prices.

Trattoria Do Forni
Calle dei Specchieri; tel: 041-523 2148; €€€; vaporetto: San Marco Giardinetti; map p.138 B2
An upmarket spot masquerading as a trattoria. Reliable cuisine and rambling yet intimate rooms. The menu embraces caviar, oysters, steak and pasta, seafood risotto and Venetian vegetable pie.

Canale Grande

Club del Doge
Hotel Gritti Palace, Campo Santa Maria del Giglio, San Marco; tel: 041-794 611; €€€; vaporetto:

San Marco and Castello sesteries are home to some of the most prestigious restaurants. Further afield, choices are more varied, and prices lower. But don't ignore the glamorous spots; Venetians patronise them too.

Al Graspo De Ua
Calle dei Bombaseri; tel: 041-520 0150; closed Sun; €€–€€€; vaporetto: Rialto; map p.138 B3
Tucked away in the warren of streets en route to the Rialto, this well-established fish restaurant has been serving spider crab, scallops and *tagliolini* with lobster since 1855.

Harry's Bar
Calle Vallaresso; tel: 041-528 5777; €€€; vaporetto: San Marco Vallaresso; map p.138 B1
The fresh, consistent menu of this legendary bar attracts wealthy Venetians as well as visitors. The tone is perfect, set by the current Arrigo (Harry) Cipriani. Guests should refrain from wearing strong perfumes or using mobile phones. Booking essential.
SEE ALSO BARS AND CAFÉS P.31

Osteria Ai Assassini
Rio Terrà degli Assassini; tel: 041-528 7986; closed Sun; €€; vaporetto: S. Angelo; map p.137 E3
A lively pub-like place with great soups. Baked fish and seafood dishes are the best choices here; *cappe sante al pomodoro* (scallops with tomato) come highly recommended.

De Pisis
Hotel Bauer, Campo San Moisè; tel: 041-520 7022; €€€; vaporetto: San Marco Vallaresso; map p.138 B1
Dazzling damask and candle-

Below: Club del Doge Restaurant in the Hotel Gritti Palace, an elegant place to dine, with one of the best terraces in the city.

Above: dining beside the Accademia Bridge.

S. M. Del Giglio; map p.138 A1
This has traditional cuisine in a palatial setting overlooking the Grand Canal, with probably the best terrace in town; equally atmospheric for lunch, drinks or a fish-based dinner. You will find that the service has a lighter touch than in most other grand hotels.

La Cusina
Hotel Westin Europa & Regina, Corte Barozzi, off Calle Larga XX11 Marzo, San Marco; tel: 041-240 0001; €€€; vaporetto: San Marco Vallaresso; map p.138 A1
International, Italian and Venetian cuisine in an elegant setting, typified by the lovely terrace and a Murano chandelier-hung interior made intimate by views of the chefs at work. One of the better grand hotel restaurants. Booking is advisable.

Hotel Monaco and Grand Canal
Calle Vallaresso, San Marco; tel 041-520 0211; €€€; vaporetto: San Marco Vallaresso; map p.138 B1

This elegant terrace restaurant (with piano bar) has fine views over the lagoon, taking in La Salute and San Giorgio. International, Italian and Venetian dishes include fish soup, vegetable risotto and scampi. Booking required.

Castello

All'Aciugheta
Campo Santi Filippo e Giacomo; tel: 041-522 4292; €€; vaporetto: S. Zaccaria Jolanda; map p.139 C2
This unpretentious, value-for-money *bacaro* goes against type by having space, a terrace and a proper menu with plenty of choice. It's popular with Venetians, tempted by the fine Friuli wines, Adriatic fish, oysters, and cheeses.

La Corte Sconta
Calle del Pestrin; tel: 041-522 7024; closed Sun and Mon; €€€; vaporetto: Arsenale; map p.139 D2
This is a renowned yet authentic venue, tucked into a secret courtyard, with a

> The house wine – *vino della casa* – is usually perfectly acceptable, and often very pleasant. It is likely to be a dry white Tocai or a red Cabernet or Merlot, all from the Friuli region to the north of Venice.

cheerful atmosphere and a menu based on fish fresh from Chioggia market. You can tuck into fishy antipasti, from scallops and *calamari* to sea snails, shrimps and sardines. Booking is advisable.

Enoteca Mascareta
Calle Lunga Santa Maria Formosa; tel: 041-523 0744; open D only (7pm–2am); €€; vaporetto: Rialto; map p.139 C3
A cosy, rustic wine-bar, run by wine writer Mauro Lorenzon. You can have salami, ham at the counter, or opt for the menu, including bean soup, lasagne and fish at the table. The convivial host, laid-back jazz and the superb wines ensure a contented clientele.

Right: café on the *campo* behind Santa Maria della Salute.

Hostaria da Franz
Fondamenta San Giuseppe (San Isepe); tel: 041-522 0861; closed Tue; €€€; vaporetto: Giardini; map p.140 B3

This quaint canal-side trattoria was opened in 1842 by an Austrian soldier who fell in love with a Venetian girl. Sample Venetian seafood dishes with a twist, from risotto to gnocchi with prawns and spinach, marinated prawns, grilled fish, or fish with polenta. It's off the beaten track, but convenient for the Biennale gardens. Booking is advisable.

Do Leoni
Hotel Londra Palace, Riva degli Schiavoni; tel: 041-520 0533; €€€; vaporetto: S. Zaccaria Jolanda; map p.139 C2

The waterfront restaurant maintains its Venetian character while satisfying international tastes. Fans of Venetian food with a contemporary twist can sample *sarde in saor* and *risi e bisi* as well as seafood grills and gnocchi with shrimps.

Above: boat delivering fresh fish to the Rialto market – Venice is noted for top-quality seafood.

There's an informal mood on the terrace. Live music in the evenings.
SEE ALSO HOTELS, P.62

Osteria Al Mascaron
Calle Lunga Santa Maria Formosa; tel: 041-522 5995; closed Sun; €€; vaporetto: Rialto; map p.139 C2

Set in a lively area, this is an ideal introduction to a Venetian inn. An old-fashioned, gentrified-rustic wine bar and inn, it offers friendly but leisurely service, fine wines and reliable cooking. Try the fresh antipasti, the bean soup, and the mixed grill; and save room for the delicious Burano biscuits dipped in dessert wine.

Osteria di Santa Marina
Campo Santa Marina; tel: 041-528 5239; closed all Sun and Mon L; €€€; vaporetto: Rialto; map p.138 B3

Set in a quiet square, this welcoming restaurant presents reinterpretations of dishes from the Veneto, from cuttlefish ink ravioli with sea bass, seafood pasta to fresh turbot, tuna, and beef carpaccio to tuna-and-bean soup and mixed grills; in summer, sit outside on the square and end the experience with a sorbet or cinnamon apple pie.

Da Remigio
Salizzada dei Greci; tel: 041-523 0089; closed Mon D and all Tue; €€; vaporetto: Pieta; map p.139 D2

This used to be a simple trattoria. It is still a local favourite but no longer a secret. Set in a newly revitalised area, the authentic menu includes meat and grilled fish, and gnocchi is a house speciality. Service can be slow but the welcome is genuine and friendly. Book in advance.

Alla Rivetta
Ponte San Provolo; tel: 041-528 7302; closed Mon; €€; vaporetto: S. Zaccaria Jolanda; map p.139 C2

Set by the bridge across the Rio del Vin, linking Campo Santi Filippo e Giacomo and Campo San Provolo, this is an unpretentious, un-touristy place close to San Marco. Fish and seafood predominate (grills and cuttlefish), as do polenta and plates of roast vegetables. Trade is brisk, the atmosphere breezy and service a touch brusque.

Prices for an average three course meal with wine:	
€	under €30
€€	€30–€55
€€€	over €50

Above: La Terrazza, the rooftop restaurant of the Hotel Danieli, a top-class establishment with an enchanting view of the lagoon.

La Terrazza
Hotel Danieli, Riva degli Schiavoni; tel: 041-522 6480; €€€; vaporetto: San Zaccaria; map p.139 C2

The view alone is worth it: the rooftop terrace of this historic hotel overlooks St Mark's Basin. Highlights of the Mediterranean-inspired cuisine are the *antipasti*, chosen from the buffet, the fish soup and the seafood. You need to book.

Dai Tosi
Seco Marina; tel: 041-523 7102; closed Wed; €; vaporetto: Giardini; map p.140 B3

As a rare outpost in eastern Castello, this dependable pizzeria and trattoria (try the spaghetti with scampi) is convenient for the Biennale gardens.

Trattoria Giorgione
Via Garibaldi; tel 041-522 8727; closed Wed; €€; vaporetto: Giardini; map p.140 A3

Set in the working-class Arsenale area of Eastern Castello, this inn is popular with Venetians, both for the traditional fish recipes and for the live folk-music most evenings.

Cannaregio

Da Alberto
Calle Giacinto Gallina; tel: 041-523 8153; closed Sun; €€; vaporetto: Rialto; map p.138 C4

Set close to the Miracoli church, this authentic *osteria* (inn) is a cosy and romantic place to sample pasta, risotto, cuttlefish and a full range of *cichetti*.

Anice Stellato
Fondamenta della Sensa; tel: 041-720 744; closed Mon and Tue; €€; vaporetto: S. Alvise; map p.135 C4

This small, family-run restaurant is a long way from the centre but always busy with

locals. You can come here just for the *cichetti* but full meals are also served.

Bentigodi-Osteria da Andrea
Calleselle; tel: 041-716 269; closed Sun; €; vaporetto: Guglie; map p.135 C3

A cheery *bacaro*, lined with wooden tables, serving a good selection of *cichetti* from aubergine nibbles to chickpea soup, seafood salad and pasta with swordfish.

Fiaschetteria Toscana
Salizzada San Giovanni Cristostomo; tel: 041-528 5281; closed Mon L and all Tue; €€€; vaporetto: Rialto; map p.138 B4

Set near the Rialto Bridge, this is a favourite among

> San Polo and Santa Croce have a few stylish restaurants, but they are among the best areas for traditional and authentic trattorie and bacari, where you can sample local food with local people.

Prices for an average three course meal with wine:	
€	under €30
€€	€30–€55
€€€	over €50

A restaurant bill may include service *(servizio)* of between 10 and 15 per cent, but ask if you're not sure. It is normal to round the bill up slightly in addition to this provided you have been happy with the service. Another extra which appears on most restaurant bills is the *'coperto'* or cover charge, which ranges from 2–6 euros.

Above: tempting freshly baked treats in a Rialto *pasticceria*.

local gourmets for excellent, good-value fish and seafood; there is also a smattering of Tuscan steak dishes and cheeses, accompanied by fine wines. Book.

Al Fontego dei Pescaori
Calle Priuli; tel: 041 520 0538; closed Mon; €€; vaporetto: Ca' d'Oro; map p.135 D2
Lolo, the owner, is president of the Rialto fish market and has his own stall, so you can guarantee the fish will be wonderfully fresh. The wide selection of seafood includes an elegantly presented platter of raw fish, grilled cuttlefish served with white polenta, scallops, sea bass and deep-fried mixed fish.

Ai Promessi Sposi
Calle dell'Oca; tel: 041-522 8609; closed Wed; €; vaporetto: Ca' d'Oro; map p.135 E1
This busy *bacaro* serves a wide selection of *cichetti*, plus clams, pasta and *pastic-*

cio di crespelle al pesce (fish pancakes) and *castraure* (baby artichokes).

Alla Vedova
Ramo Ca' d'Oro; tel: 041-528 5324; closed Thur and Sun L; €; vaporetto: Ca' d'Oro; map p.135 D2
Set near the Ca' d'Oro, this friendly and reliable *bacaro* is popular with young Venetians who cluster around the bar to sample such tapas as *polpette* (spicy meatballs), *baccalà*, fried artichokes, marinated peppers, or seafood, including cuttlefish gnocchi with salmon. There's table service too.

Vini da Gigio
Fondamenta di San Felice; tel: 041-528 5140; closed Mon and Tue; €€; vaporetto: Ca' d'Oro; map p.135 D2
A very popular family-run *bacaro* that is both a wine bar and inn, with excep-

tional food but leisurely service. There's lots of variety, from Venetian risotto to northern Italian game dishes, as well as fine wines. Booking advisable.

San Polo

Antiche Carampane
Rio Terrà delle Carampane; tel: 041-524 0165; closed Sun–Mon; €€; vaporetto: Rialto; map p.137 E4
Not easy to find, but worth the search because the seafood dishes are excellent, even if the service can be a bit brusque. You can eat at tables outside in summer.

Al Bancogiro
Campo San Giacometto; tel: 041-523 2061; closed Sun D and Mon; €€; vaporetto: Rialto; map p.138 B3
Fitting snugly into ancient porticoes by the busy Rialto crossing, this fashionable wine bar and new-wave *bacaro* stands on the site of the city's earliest bank. Eat *cichetti* with locals at the bustling bar or terrace; or select from the short but ever-changing menu upstairs, with dishes based on fresh produce from the nearby fish and vegetable markets.

Da Fiore
Calle del Scaleter, off Campo di San Polo; tel: 041-721 308;

Below: shrimps from the lagoon.

Left: Ai Gondolieri, a popular restaurant near the Guggenheim Museum.

lunchtime on Saturday for huge portions of *fritto misto* (deep-fried fish) laid out on a large table in the Campo. During the week it's popular for early evening aperitifs, as well as the creative range of fish dishes.

Al Nono Risorto
Sottoportego della Siora Bettina, Campo San Cassiano; tel: 041-524 1169; closed Wed; €€; vaporetto: San Silvestro; map p.137 D4
A rustic spot, framed by a wisteria-hung courtyard and garden is popular with 30-something Venetians. A combination of pizzeria and trattoria, it offers a changing menu of fish, pasta and pizzas.

Da Pinto
Campo delle Beccarie; tel: 041-522 4599; closed Mon; €; vaporetto: Rialto; map p.134 A4
This historic Rialto market inn has been restored, revealing a huge fireplace in the medieval meathouse. Snooty local people say the *osteria* has sold out by offering pizza, but they still serve *cichetti* at the bar or a generous menu (pasta, fish grill and dessert for around €20). You can eat seated beneath exposed beams or outside on the market square.

Santa Croce

Antica Bessetta
Salizzada de Ca' Zusto; tel: 041-721 687; closed all Tue and Wed L; €€; vaporetto: R. D. Biasio; map p.134 B1
Off the beaten track, just north of San Giacomo dell'Orio, this is a rustic-style trattoria, but standards, and prices, are high. It is a temple of Venetian home cooking and a foodies' paradise, with

closed Sun and Mon; €€€; vaporetto: S. Toma; map p.136 C4
Possibly the best restaurant in town, and a celebrity haunt during the Film Festival. Local people claim that Da Fiore is an accurate reflection of the subtlety of Venetian cuisine, from grilled *calamari* and *granseola* (spider crab) to Adriatic tuna, squid, sashimi and *risotto al nero di seppia* (cuttlefish risotto). Only one (much sought-after) table overlooks the canal.

Frary's
Fondamenta dei Frari; tel: 041-720 050; closed Tue; €; vaporetto: S. Toma; map p.137 C4
Facing the Frari church, this

cosy, reliable Arab and Greek restaurant aspires to a 'thousand-and-one-nights' atmosphere. Dishes run from Greek salad and moussaka to an array of Lebanese *mezze* (a selection of small dishes) and fish couscous.

Alla Madonna
Calle della Madonna; tel: 041-522 3824; closed Wed; €€; vaporetto: Rialto; map p.138 A3
Tucked away down a tiny canal just beyond the Rialto bank, this is a reliable and ever-popular old inn that specialises in Venetian cuisine, from seafood risotto to polenta and spider crab. The service is brisk and animated, but expect to queue along with chatty local people.

Al Muro
Campo Bella Vienna; tel: 041-523 7495; closed Sun; €€; vaporetto: Rialto; map p.137 E4
Venetians flock here at

Prices for an average three course meal with wine:	
€	under €30
€€	€30–€55
€€€	over €50

risi e bisi (rice and peas), gnocchi, seafood risotto; or the catch of the day, grilled or baked, accompanied by distinctive regional wines.

Il Refolo
Campiello del Piovan, off Campo San Giacomo dell'Orio; tel: 041-524 0016; closed all Mon and Tue L; €€; vaporetto: R. D. Biasio; map p.134 C1

In a pretty canalside setting, this innovative, upmarket pizzeria is a great place for a peaceful meal. There are classic as well as creative pizzas.

Alla Zucca
Ponte del Megio; tel: 041-524 1570; closed Sun and all Aug; €€; vaporetto: S. Stae; map p.135 C1

This is an extremely popular trattoria, set by a crooked bridge over the canal, with a few tables outside when the weather is warm. The bohemian atmosphere reflects the eclectic menu, which favours vegetables as well as fish, with creamy pumpkin flan (*zucca* means pumpkin), aubergine pasta and smoked mackerel. You should book in advance.

> If you are planning a trip to Venice in August bear in mind that the majority of restaurants are closed, either for the whole month or at least a good part of it.

Dorsoduro
La Bitta
Calle Lunga San Barnaba; tel: 041-523 0531; closed Sun; €€; vaporetto: Ca Rezzonico; map p.136 B2

An unpretentious little restaurant which, unusually for Venice, concentrates on meat dishes; in fact, no fish at all. Steak, chicken and *fegato alla veneziana* (calves' liver with onions) are all served, and are very good value.

Cantinone già Schiavi
Fondamenta Nani, Rio di San Trovaso; tel: 041-523 0034; closes 9.30pm and Sun D; €; vaporetto: Zattece; map p.137 B2

This old-fashioned canalside wine bar is popular with local people and expats from all walks of life. It's a good place for *cichetti*. Savour the mood by popping in for a light lunch at the bar or lingering at the cocktail hour (7–8pm).

La Furatola
Calle Lunga San Barnaba; tel: 041-520 8294; closed Thur; €€; vaporetto: Ca Rezzonico; map p.136 B2

A cosy place renowned for its fresh fish, ample portions of pasta (often big enough to share, a practice that is not frowned on), and wonderful desserts.

Ai Gondolieri
Ponte del Formager; tel: 041-528 6396; closed Tue; €€€; vaporetto: Salute; map p.137 D1

Set close to the Guggenheim this stylish modern restaurant eschews fish and thrives on a meaty menu, supported by exceptional risotto and good vegetable dishes; try the stuffed baked courgettes (*zucchini*). You are advised to book.

Linea d'Ombra
Ponte dell'Umiltà, Zattere; tel: 041-241 1881; closed Wed; €€€; vaporetto: Salute; map p.137 E1

Facing the Il Redentore church on the Giudecca, this

> Menus are often shorter and less expensive at midday.

Below: minimalist interior of the Linea d'Ombra.

romantic restaurant and wine bar is perfect on a summer's evening. It serves reinterpreted Venetian classics, with fresh fish and good wines. Booking essential in summer.

Da Montin
Fondamenta delle Eremite; tel: 041-522 7151; closed Tue D and Wed; €€€; vaporetto: Zattece; map p.136 B2

This enchanting but overpriced arty garden restaurant was once favoured by such luminaries as Hemingway and Peggy Guggenheim. Although it is most popular in summer, the cosy, faintly bohemian dining room comes into its own in winter.

Quatro Feri
Calle Lunga San Barnaba; tel: 041-520 6978; closed Sun; €€; vaporetto: Ca Rezzonico; map p.136 C2

This bustling new-wave

bacaro has a youthful owner, Barbara, and her reasonable prices attract a faithful young crowd to sample Venetian dishes. As befits a former sommelier, Barbara serves superior wines.

Giudecca and San Giorgio Maggiore Islands

Altanella
Calle delle Erbe; tel: 041-522 7780; closed Mon and Tue; no credit cards; €€–€€€; vaporetto: Redatore; map p.22

Friendly trattoria favoured by Elton John, who has a home around the corner. Only fish dishes on offer.

Fortuny Restaurant
Hotel Cipriani, Fondamenta San Giovanni; tel: 041-520 7744; closed Nov–March; €€€; vaporetto: Zitelle; map p.22

Set in the city's most luxurious hotel, the Fortuny spills

Prices for an average three course meal with wine:	
€	under €30
€€	€30–€55
€€€	over €50

onto a glorious terrace. The setting is exquisite, the service divine and the prices deadly. Or try the more informal Cip's Club (prices are lower, but still high). Both offer rare views across to San Marco and free launch service from St Mark's pier. You need to book ahead.

Harry's Dolci
Fondamenta San Biagio; tel: 041-522 4844; closed Tue and Nov–Feb; €€€; vaporetto: S. Eufemia; map p.22

Pop over to Harry's Dolci for a waterside American brunch; it's 'Harry's without the hype', but with better views and prices. Try the Venetian risotto, curried chicken or baccalà mantecato, and sip a signature Bellini in the bar. Tasty pastries are served outside mealtimes.

Do Mori
Fondamenta Sant'Eufemia; tel: 041-522 5452; closed Sun; €€; vaporetto: S. Eufemia; map p.22

Formed by a breakaway group from Harry's Bar, this is the place for those who can't afford the elevated prices of the original. The food is sound Venetian home-cooking, with a preponderance of fish dishes (try the scampi risotto) as well as pasta and pizzas.

Murano and Burano

Ai Frati
Fondamenta Venier, Murano; tel: 041-736 694; closed Thur; €€–€€€; vaporetto: Murano; map p.24

This is Murano's best fish restaurant. If you have the choice, try to get one of the tables on a mooring platform

Below: Quatro Feri, one of a new generation of reasonably priced *bacari*.

Above: the chic Liberty Restaurant, in the Lido's historic Hôtel des Bains.

on the canal. The location and neighbourhood bistro atmosphere make it very popular, so be sure to book.

Ai Pescatori
Piazza Galuppi, Burano; tel: 041-730 650; closed Wed; €€; vaporetto: Burano; map p.24

This welcoming restaurant serves fish and game. Try the seafood risotto or tagliolini with cuttlefish (*seppie*).

Da Romano
Via Galuppi, Burano; tel: 041-730 030; closed Sun D and Tue; €€; vaporetto: Burano; map p.24

A long-established restaurant is set in the island's former lace school; the interior is lit by glass lamps and adorned with paintings donated by visiting artists.

Trattoria Busa alla Torre
Campo Santo Stefano, 3, Murano; tel: 041-739 662; L only; €€; vaporetto: Murano; map p.24

This classic Venetian fish and seafood restaurant has been an inn since 1420 and a wine-store for even longer; since the 12th century, in fact. Clams, fish grills and lagoon vegetables are among the many culinary delights on offer.

The Lido

Liberty Restaurant
Hôtel des Bains, Lungomare Marconi, 17; tel: 041-526 5921; €€€; vaporetto: Lido; map p.26

This Art Deco restaurant, decorated with classical frescoes and Murano glass chandeliers, is perfectly pleasant, but the opulent setting is more impressive than the food. There is an additional beach restaurant as well as buffets and snacks served around the pool.

La Taverna
Hotel Westin Excelsior, Lungomare Marconi 41; tel: 041-526 0201; €€€; vaporetto: Lido; map p.26

This summery restaurant spreads out under an attractive terrace overlooking the beach. There is a very good buffet with a range of delicious grilled fish. You should book.

Venetians eat earlier than people in many other Italian cities. Although late-night dining is becoming more popular, in most restaurants it is advisable to arrive for dinner by around 8.30pm.

San Clemente

Hotel San Clemente Palace
Tel: 041-244 5001; €€€; ferry: San Clemente

This former monastery is now a luxury hotel with three restaurants. Ca' dei Frati is the most enchanting, with views across to San Marco, while La Laguna is a casual poolside affair. There's a free private launch from St Mark's.
SEE ALSO HOTELS, P.65

Torcello

Locanda Cipriani
Piazza Santa Fosca 29; tel: 041-730 150; closed Tue, and Jan; €€€; ferry: Torcello

This remote but lovely inn run by the nephew of Arrigo Cipriani, the owner of Harry's Bar, is a local institution. Try the grilled fish, fillet steak or *risotto alla Torcellana*. You need to book.

Al Ponte del Diavolo
Torcello 10; tel: 041-730 401; L only, closed Mon and Jan–Feb; €€; ferry: Torcello

A great atmosphere and efficient service in this pleasant rustic lunch venue. Pasta and seafood are specialities.

115

Sculpture

Sculptors in Renaissance Venice were often master craftsmen, working on the design and architecture of a building as well as embellishing it with sculptural details. The Lombardi family, for example, were the designers of churches and palazzi, as well as leading sculptors who carved tombs for doges, and decorated church and palace façades. The reluctance to glorify anything beyond the Serenissima led to a sparsity of free-standing statues in the city. The notable exception is Verrocchio's magnificent monument to Colleoni in the Campo Santi Giovanni e Paolo whose church houses some of the finest sculpture in the city.

Bartolomeo Bon (c.1405–1467)

This prolific Venetian sculptor and architect designed the **Porta della Carta**, the ceremonial gateway of the **Doge's Palace**. Above the portal is the sculpted figure of Doge Francesco Foscari who commissioned the gateway, kneeling before the winged lion. Bon also worked on the **Ca' d'Oro**, and on the portals of the churches of **Santi Giovanni e Paolo** and **Madonna dell'Orto**.
SEE ALSO CHURCHES, P.41–3; PALAZZI, P.93, 97

The Lombardi (1435–1532)

Pietro Lombardo (c.1435–1516) and his sons, Tullio (c.1455–1532) and Antonio (1458–1516), collaborated on many works and are often known collectively as the Lombardi. Pietro was born in Cremona, trained as a sculptor in Rome, then transferred with his sons to the Veneto in 1460. To see some of their great masterpieces visit the **Church of Santi Giovanni e Paolo**, which houses Pietro's

Above: Scala del Gigante, the VIP entrance to the Palazzo Ducale.

magnificent *Monument to Doge Nicolò Marcello* (1474) and *Tomb of Pietro Mocenigo* (1481) and Tullio's *Tomb of Andrea Vendramin* (c.1493). There is a delightful *Last Supper* of Carrara marble in Santa Maria dei Miracoli by Tullio and a beautiful sculpted portrait of a young couple in the **Franchetti Gallery** (Ca' D'Oro). It is said that Tullio was the first sculptor to achieve

correct Classical proportions. The talented family also diversified into architecture, and excelled themselves in designing two Venetian gems: the church of **Santa Maria dei Miracoli** and the **Ca'Dario** on the Grand Canal. They were also responsible for decorating the sumptuous marble lower section of Coducci's façade of the **Scuola Grande di San Marco**.
SEE ALSO CHURCHES, P.41, 42; MUSEUMS AND GALLERIES, P.78; PALAZZI, P.100; SCUOLE, P.118–9

Andrea del Verrocchio (1435–88)

A follower of Donatello, Verrocchio was one of the leading sculptors of the day and his equestrian statue of Bartolommeo Colleoni (begun 1481, completed after his death) ranks among the great masterpieces of Italian sculpture. Colleoni (1400-76) was a celebrated *condottiere* (mercenary soldier) and his bequest to the city came with a stipulation that a monument be erected to him on St Mark's Square. The authorities cunningly relegated the idealised

Renaissance statue to the lesser spot outside the Scuola di San Marco, in the Campo di Santi Giovanni e Paolo.

Jacopo Sansovino (1486–1570)

This fine Mannerist sculptor and architect took his name from his Tuscan master, Andrea Sansovino (1467–1529). He fled the Sack of Rome in 1527 and came to Venice where he quickly adapted to the Venetian sensibility despite his Tuscan background and Roman training. In his role as Superintendent of the Works, he became the city's leading architect. The best-known of his sculptures are the huge figures of *Mars and Neptune* (over 3m high) on the stairs of the **Palazzo Ducale**, on which he worked between 1554 and 1566. His sensitive Carrara marble *Madonna and Child* was

designed for the now-deconsecrated Zitelle church. You can see his bronze *Allegory of the Redemption* in the **Basilica di San Marco**; and *St John the Baptist*, dating from 1554, in the **Frari**. Successfully fusing architecture with sculpture, he designed the Loggetta – the classical loggia at the base of the Campanile in the Piazza San Marco – in red, white and green marble. It was destroyed when the tower collapsed in 1902, but subsequently rebuilt. He is most

Left: Canova's tomb, the Frari.

famous for his design of the **Librera Marciana**, the national library, also known as the Libreria Sansoviniana.
SEE ALSO CHURCHES, P.38, 43; PALAZZI, P.93

Antonio Canova (1757–1822)

The great Neoclassical sculptor, famous for his marble nudes, was born in the village of Possagno in the Veneto. As a boy, he came to the attention of the Venetian senator, Giovanni Falier, who became his patron; he was then apprenticed to sculptor Giuseppi Bernardi. Canova's best-known works in Venice are the sculpted *Baskets of Fruit* (1772), *Euridice and Orfeo* (1773–76) and *Dedalo and Icaro* (1777–79), all displayed in the Neoclassical rooms of the **Museo Correr**. The sculptor's mausoleum is in the **Frari** church. He designed it as a tomb for Titian, but after his death his pupils used the design for their master's monument. The sinister, open-doored pyramid contains the sculptor's heart.
SEE ALSO CHURCHES, P.43; MUSEUMS AND GALLERIES, P.75

Below: Bartolommeo Colleoni, by Andrea del Verrocchio.

Scuole

Dating back to the Middle Ages, the *scuole* were charitable lay associations close to the heart of Venetian life. Until the fall of the Republic at the end of the 18th century they acted as a state within a state, looking after members' spiritual, moral and material welfare. Although secular, the *scuole* were devotional associations. The members of these confraternities prayed together and performed charitable works in the name of their patron saint. All scuole wished to glorify their patron saint and themselves by employing the great artists of the day to decorate the interiors of their meeting houses.

Scuole Distinctions and Similarities

While there were great distinctions between the prestigious *scuole grandi* and the humble *scuole minori* they were essentially democratic associations, with rich and poor people able to join at different rates of subscription. The *scuole grandi* possessed great wealth and prestige, and played a leading role in the ceremonial life of the city. These include San Rocco, San Giovanni Evangelista, I Carmini, San Marco and Santa Maria della Carità; the latter now home to the Accademia gallery, which houses pre-1800s art.

There were also associations for foreign communities, such as the Scuola di San Giorgio degli Schiavoni, intended for workers from Dalmatia – present-day Croatia.

Corporate funds were lavished on the grand interiors of meeting houses and the great artists who had decorated the Doge's Palace were employed to adorn them. Set on two floors and linked by a magnificent

Above: Scuola di San Giorgio degli Schiavoni, well known for its paintings by Carpaccio.

staircase, a typical headquarters had halls decorated by the finest artists of the age, rich in narrative scenes and in dazzling processions.

By the 18th century there were almost 500 confraternities. Although Napoleon sacked their headquarters and disbanded the confraternities in 1806, several have since been revived and still more former meeting houses are now open to the public.

Some of the *scuole* have become permanent museums or regular concert halls. One is now a school sports hall, and the Scuola Grande di San Marco *(see below)* is home to the city hospital.

The *scuole* are concentrated in the areas of Castello, San Polo, Santa Croce and Dorsoduro.

Castello

Scuola Grande di San Marco
Fondamenta dei Mendicanti; vaporetto: Ospedale Civile; map p.139 D4

Formerly a goldsmiths' and silk merchants' philanthropic confraternity, this was once the richest Venetian Scuola, but is now mired in long-term renovation. It was built in the late-15th century to replace the first confraternity which was destroyed by fire. The marble façade, only partially visible, has weathered badly in the damp Venetian climate. The confraternity retains its *trompe l'oeil* Renaissance façade as well as its assembly rooms and chapter house. In keeping with the

Left: The Assumption of the Virgin, one of the many works by Tintoretto in the Scuola di San Rocco.

have survived in the building for which it was painted.

Carpaccio's vibrant works are displayed in a mysterious, intimate setting, below a coffered ceiling. They are characterised by dramatic storytelling. In particular, the *St George and the Dragon* paintings are bold chivalric scenes with a captivating depiction of a knight in shining armour, a dying dragon and a place of desolation, with the ground littered with skulls, vipers and vultures. Equally beguiling is the St Jerome trilogy, with *The Miracle of the Lion* showing the saint extracting a thorn from the lion's paw. *The Vision of St Jerome*, rendered in meticulous detail, is both one of the most engaging works and his masterpiece, conveying a mood of contemplative calm and a Tuscan sense of space combined with Flemish realism.

Below: doorway of the Scuola di San Giovanni Evangelista.

The Scuola Grande di San Teodoro overlooking the Campo San Salvador (San Marco) was built in the mid-17th century, the last of the *scuole grande*. A spacious building on two floors, it is now only open for concerts, when singers and orchestra appear in 18th-century costume (tel: 041-521 8294 for tickets).

charitable aims of the confraternity, it is fitting that the city hospital should now be based here.

A grand portal framed by illusionistic lions leads into the hushed hospital, with the foyer now occupying the cloisters of the former Dominican foundation. Although there is no official public entrance to the Scuola you can glimpse the entrance hall, slip past reception and walk upstairs to check the current opening times (they seem to vary quite a lot) posted on the door of the medical library, housed in the panelled, 16th-century assembly rooms.

Scuola di San Giorgio degli Schiavoni

Calle dei Furlani; tel: 041-522 8828; Apr–Oct: Tue–Sat 9.30am–12.30pm and 3.30–6.30pm, Sun 9.30am–12.30pm, Nov–Mar: Tue–Sat 10am–12.30pm and 3–6pm, Sun 10am–12.30pm; entrance charge; vaporetto: San Zaccaria; map p.139 D3

The loveliest confraternity seat in Venice. The Scuola was intended to protect the interests of Slavs from Dalmatia (Schiavonia), the first Venetian colony. On the completion of the building in 1501, the confraternity commissioned Venetian-born artist Vittorio Carpaccio (1460–1525) to execute a painting cycle in honour of the Dalmatian patron saints, St George, St Tryphon and St Jerome. The paintings were originally intended to decorate the upper hall, but were transferred to ground level when the Scuola was reconstructed in the mid-16th century. Despite remodelling, the Scuola retains its authentic atmosphere and has the only Venetian pictorial cycle to

Scuola Grande di San Rocco

Campo San Rocco, San Polo; tel: 041-523 4864; Apr–Oct: 9am–5.30pm; Nov–Mar: 10am–5pm; entrance charge; vaporetto: San Tomà; map p.136 C4;

One of the greatest city sights, and the grandest of the *scuole*, today San Rocco acts as a backdrop for Baroque recitals. The society is dedicated to St Roch, the French patron saint of plague victims, who so impressed the Venetians that they stole his relics and canonised him.

The 16th-century building is also a shrine to Tintoretto, the great Mannerist painter, whose pictorial cycle adorns the walls. He won a competition to decorate the interior; clinched by his cunning submission of a perfectly completed panel rather than the requested cartoon. He worked on the Scuola on and off for 24 years. Hand-held mirrors are provided to help view the ceiling paintings; even so, most visitors will find they suffer vertigo and sensory overload. His overpowering biblical scenes (1564–87), provoke strong responses. New Testament scenes are displayed in the *sala inferiore* (ground floor hall), including *The Annunciation*, a dramatic *chiaroscuro* composition. Such works show the painter's profound Biblical knowledge and manipulation of Mannerist iconography. According to art historian Bernard Berenson 'the poetry which quickens most of his works is almost entirely a matter of light and colour.'

A gilded staircase leads to the *sala grande* (great upper hall), and the *sala dell'*

San Polo

Scuola Grande di San Giovanni Evangelista

Calle de la Laca, San Polo; tel: 041-718 234; open for concerts or by prior appointment; vaporetto: San Tomà; map p.136 C4

The Scuola still serves its original purpose, so it's difficult to gain access, but worth seeing from outside. The distinctive Renaissance marble portal and courtyard is watched over by an eagle, the symbol of St John, the confraternity's patron saint. The interior is graced by a monumental staircase, a barrel-vaulted, double-ramp affair, but most of the finest paintings are now in the Accademia (see p.81–2).

In San Rocco, the writer Henry James found 'the air thick with genius' yet palpably human: 'It is not immortality that we breathe at San Rocco but conscious, reluctant mortality.'

Albergo (smaller assembly room). This upper floor is framed by an inlaid marble floor and by surfaces studded with one of the finest painting cycles imaginable. Tintoretto's genius is revealed in these dynamic orchestrations of colour and light, works marked by drama and strong composition.

The *sala grande* uses telling biblical scenes to accentuate the confraternity's mission to heal. Stagily set on easels by the altar are Tiepolo's *Abraham and the Angels* and Titian's poetic *Annunciation*, matched by his *Christ Carrying the Cross*. The Sala dell'Albergo contains allegories linked to the society's patron saint, including *St Roch in Glory*, the ceiling panel that won Tintoretto the entire commission. Facing you as you enter the room is *The Crucifixion*, a vast masterpiece with a charged atmosphere and a poignant drama.

Dorsoduro

Scuola Grande dei Carmini

Campo dei Carmini; tel: 041-528 9420; Mon–Sat 9am–4pm; Sun 9am–1pm; also hosts classical concerts; entrance charge; vaporetto: San Basilio; map p.136 B3

The headquarters of the Carmelite order, this is one of the city's grandest confraternities, at least in artistic terms. The uninspired façade, built by Longhena, conceals a lavish 18th-century interior.

The ground floor comprises a frescoed great hall

and sacristy. A monumental twin staircase, its barrel-vaulted ceilings encrusted with stuccowork, leads to a splendid showcase to Tiepolo. On the left is the *sala dell'albergo* (lodging room), which housed pilgrims, and the *sala dell'archivio*, where the confraternity archives were stored. The decoration of the *salone* (assembly room) on the right was entrusted to Tiepolo. Since the wealthy order prospered during the Counter-reformation, with the cult of Mary acting as a counterweight to Protestantism, the Carmelites could afford to summon the services of the greatest Rococo painter. Tiepolo repaid their confidence with a series of sensuous masterpieces, a floating world of pale skies and illusionistic effects. In the centre of the ceiling is a visionary work showing the *Virgin with the Blessed Simon Stock*. Tradition has it that Stock had

a vision of the Virgin bestowing the Carmelites with their sacred badge, the scapular. It is said that the Carmelites were so pleased with it they made Tiepolo an honorary member of the Scuola.

As the order was re-established during the 13th century, Stock became one of the first Englishmen to join. He led the Carmelites during the time of their realignment to the Mendicant Friars and remained at their head for 20 years, writing several hymns and decrees for the order.

The corners of the ceiling are graced by four voluptuous *Virtues*, a radiant allegorical work.

One of the more humble *scuole*, the Scuola dei Varotari, formerly the Tanners' Guild, still stands at the fish stall end of the lively, sprawling Campo Santa Margherita in Dorsoduro.

Below: ceiling painting by Tiepolo in the Scuola Grande dei Carmini.

Shopping

To enjoy the excitement of finding something truly Venetian, you need curiosity, conviction and a substantial budget. Venetian crafts people continue to flourish despite the more recent influx of imitations, and you don't have to look far to find fascinating small specialist shops and local artisans at work in their ateliers. Watch out for beautifully crafted Venetian masks, marbled paper, Murano glass, hand-made picture frames, lace, linen and costume jewellery. Other good buys include silk ties, leather goods (mostly made on the nearby Brenta Riviera), and lambswool and angora sweaters.

What to Buy

The best things to buy in Venice are specialist items: arts and crafts, especially luxury fabrics, glassware, marbled paper and genuine masks.

The Mercerie, which links Piazza San Marco with the Rialto, is a good place to start a shopping – or just a window-shopping – expedition. This is a busy shopping thoroughfare, comprising five surprisingly narrow streets, each one with a *merceria* or haberdashery. 'The most delicious streete in the world,' was how John Evelyn described the Mercerie in 1645. It was then the main street of Venice, its shops filled with sumptuous goods from the East: golden cloth

Above: visit one of the traditional mask shops for a made-to-measure mask.

and rich damask, tapestries and carpets, perfumes, potions and spices.

Nowadays, the parade of window displays ranges from mass-produced glittery masks and Pinocchios to stylish leather and designer shops, offering the latest fashions. The best place to start is the arch under the Torre dell'Orologio (Clock Tower) in Piazza San Marco. Work your way north along the narrow streets, following signs for the Rialto. En route you will pass jewellers, boutiques, numerous shoe

stores and a proliferation of glass shops.

Fabrics

Venice is well known for its Fortuny fabrics – silks and velvets, plain or gloriously patterned. The Spanish-born Mario Fortuny began producing jewel-coloured velvets and bold silks inspired by original Renaissance costumes in his Giudecca factory a century ago. The factory at Fondamenta San Biagio (tel: 041-522 4078) on the island still produces fabrics created according to Fortuny designs.

> Shops are traditionally open Monday to Saturday from 9am–12.30/1pm and from around 3.30–7.30pm though an increasing number are now open all day. Those aimed specifically at tourists may open on Sunday, but most stores will be closed.

Valentino, Louis Vuitton, Bruno Magli, Fendi, Moschino, Prada and Gucci; all of which have eye-catching window displays. A few places to try include:

Mario Borsato
Calle Vallaresso, San Marco; tel: 041-521 0313; vaporetto: San Marco Vallaresso; map p.137 D2
For dresses, shirts and knitwear. It's considered pretty trendy but the staff aren't too cool to be friendly and helpful.

Glass

The great names of Venetian glassware usually have outlets in central Venice, although their factories and main showrooms are on the island of Murano. Prices are no cheaper there than they are in the city, but it's better to refrain from buying glass until you have visited the Murano Glass Museum, and watched it being made at a factory, which is fascinating. Only buy glass that is guaranteed by the Vetro Artistico Murano trademark

Equally fine are the reels of velvets, damasks and brocades created by the family firm of Bevilacqua, who work on the same 18th-century wooden looms that they used when the firm first started. The following are recommended textile outlets:

Frette

Calle Larga XXII Marzo, San Marco; tel: 041-522 4914; vaporetto: Santa Maria del Giglio; map p.138 B2
Frette sell fine linens, exquisite sheets, cushions and luxury bathrobes. They recently contributed to the restoration of Ca' Foscari, acting in the long tradition of Venetian patronage.

Gaggio

Campo Santo Stefano, San Marco; tel: 041-522 8574; vaporetto: San Angelo; map p.137 D2
Gaggio is widely renowned for printing Art Deco designs on silk and velvet fabrics, with stylish results.

Jesurum

Fondamenta della Sensa, Cannaregio; tel: 041-524 2540; vaporetto: San Alvise; map p.136 C1

This classy establishment has been selling gorgeous household linen, including embroidered sheets, since 1870.

Fashion

The most elegant designer boutiques are on Calle Vallaresso, Salizzada San Moisè, the Frezzeria and Calle Larga XXII Marzo, west of San Marco. Among the big names represented are Laura Biagiotti, Versace,

Below: printed velvet with Renaissance influenced motifs, by textile designer Mario Fortuny.

Above: Murano glass.

(www.muranoglass.com), and resist the hard sell before you are sure you know what you like. Be prepared for high prices at the reputable glass producers, and, if you're brave enough, always try bargaining.

The following are some of the best places to try:

Barovier e Toso
Fondamenta Vetrai 28, Murano; tel: 041-527 4385; vaporetto: Colona; map p.24

This produces pieces in simpler taste than many of the others.

Galleria Marina Barovier
Salizzada San Samuele, San Marco; tel: 041-523 6748; vaporetto: San Samuele; map p.137 C3; Calle delle Botteghe, off Campo Santo Stefano; vaporetto: Santa Maria del Giglio; map p.137 D2

Modern and contemporary Murano glass.

Venini
Piazzetta Leoncini 314, San Marco; tel: 041-522 4045; vaporetto: San Marco Giardinetti; map p.138 B2; factory and showrooms at Fondamenta Vetrai 50, Murano; tel: 041-273 7211; vaporetto: Colona; map p.24

One of the most prestigious contemporary glassmakers. All pieces are signed and dated.

Jewellery

Genninger Studio
Calle del Traghetto, Dorsoduro next to Ca' Rezzonico; tel: 041-522 5565; vaporetto: Ca' Rezzonico; map p.137 C3

A wide assortment of beautiful hand-made glass-bead jewellery, some set in silver or 24-carat gold. Designer Leslie Genninger is often on hand to discuss the techniques she uses, and always makes customers feel welcome.

IVA (value-added tax) is added to prices on a sliding scale, reaching 19 per cent. Non-EU citizens are entitled to a refund of this tax on purchases of 180 euros or more, if made in one place; ask for an invoice from the seller. Save receipts until you leave your last EU destination. Look out for shops offering tax-free shopping for tourists, as they usually deduct this tax on the spot.

Hibiscus
Rughetta de Ravano, San Polo; tel: 041-520 8989; vaporetto: San Silvestro; map p.137 D4

The place for some lovely, and unusual hand-made jewellery and pearl necklaces.

Zaggia
Calle della Toletta, Dorsoduro; tel: 041-522 3159; vaporetto: Accademia; map p.136 C2

Nadia Viani uses tiny mosaics and pearls to create antique-style necklaces, bracelets and brooches.

Lace

The island of Burano is famous for traditional lace-making and the museum there is well worth visiting. Lace-buying, on the other hand, is not so easy. The real, hand-crafted thing is extremely expensive, because it is so labour-intensive. Much of the lace you see, in Burano and in shops around Piazza San Marco and elsewhere, is machine-made and has been imported from the Far East. Ask for proof of origin before buying.

Merletti d'Arte Martina
Via San Mauro 307-9, Burano; vaporetto: Burano; map p.24

One of the best outlets for genuine hand-made lace on Burano.

Marbled Paper

Between San Marco and the Rialto you will find shops selling marbled paper, another Venetian speciality. Called *legatoria* (book-binding) this ancient craft gives paper a decorative marbled veneer and is today used for photo albums, writing cases, greeting cards, address books, diaries and notebooks; which all make lovely and extremely portable gifts and souvenirs. Places to try include:

Karisma
San Polo, near Casa Goldoni; tel: 041-710 670; vaporetto: San Silvestro; map p.137 D4
Hand-printed books, marbled paper, photo albums, etc. All purchases are beautifully wrapped.

Legatoria Piazzesi
Campiello della Feltrina, San Marco, near Santa Maria del Giglio; tel: 041-522 1202; vaporetto: Santa Maria del Giglio; map p.137 D2

The oldest and best-known producer of hand-printed paper in Venice.

Paolo Olbi
Campo Santa Maria Nova, Cannaregio; tel: 041-523 7655; vaporetto: Rialto; map p.135 E1
Hand-crafted, leather-bound photograph albums and notebooks tooled with the shapes and symbols of historic Venice.

Masks

It is particularly good fun to visit the mask workshops in the run up to carnival, when masks are being ordered and tried on. Unless they are attending the carnival, visitors usually buy these colourful masks to adorn walls when they get home, rather than to wear.

Before buying a mask, always check what it is made of and ask the seller (if their English or your Italian is up to it) to tell you how it fits into the Venetian tradition: it may be a character from the *Commedia dell'Arte*, the 16th-century comic drama

tradition that laid the foundation for puppet shows throughout Europe, and pantomime in England.

The original masks were made either of leather or of *cartapesta* (papier-mâché) and many of them still are, if you go to the right places and avoid the cheap-and-cheerful. Some of the most genuine and appealing mask shops lie in the Castello district, in the quiet canals behind San Zaccaria. The following are authentic yet lively places that specialise in making and selling both theatrical and carnival masks:

Atelier Marega
Fondamenta dell' Osmarin, Castello; tel: 041-522 3036; vaporetto: San Zaccaria; map p.139 C2; Campo San Rocco; tel: 041-717966; vaporetto: San Tomà; map p.136 C1; San Tomà, Calle Larga Foscari; tel: 041-717 966; vaporetto: San Tomà; map p.137 C3
Gorgeous traditional masks for sale, and carnival/fancy dress costumes for hire.

Below: lighting emporium near Campo Santa Maria Formosa.

Below: hand-made lace from the island of Burano, home of fishermen and lacemakers.

Right: there's no shortage of Venetian mask shops.

Ca' del Sol
Fondamenta del Osmarin, Castello; tel: 041-528 5549; vaporetto: San Zaccharia; map p.139 C2

A group of artists who started out in the 1980s making replicas of typical masks, and creating new designs, using traditional methods. They have a workshop and a retail outlet on the same premises.

Flavia
Corte Spechiera, Castello, close to Campo Santa Marina; tel: 041-528 7429; vaporetto: San Marco Giardinetti; map p.138 B2

Flavia hires and sells full-scale carnival costumes as well as masks.

Laboratorio Artigiano Maschere
Barberie delle Tole, Castello; tel: 041-522 3110; vaporetto: Ospedale Civile; map p.139 C3

Close to the church of Santi Giovanni e Paolo, this is an old-established family firm.

Mondonovo
Rio Terrà Canal, off Campo Santa Margherita, Dorsoduro; tel: 041-528 7344; vaporetto: Ca' Rezzonico; map p.136 B3

Renowned as one of the most creative mask-makers.

Tragicomica
Calle Nomboli, San Polo; tel: 041-721 102; vaporetto: San Tomà; map p.137 C4

Masks range from *Commedia dell'Arte* characters (Harlequin, Punch, etc) to allegorical masks of the creator's own invention. Each one is handmade by craftspeople.

Paintings and Prints

Antiquus
Calle delle Botteghe, San Marco; tel: 041-520 6395; vaporetto: San Samuele; map p.137 D3

Tempting little antique-shop selling silverware, jewellery and 18th- and 19th-century paintings.

Contini
Calle dello Spezier, off Campo Santo Stefano, San Marco; tel: 041-520 4942; vaporetto: San Marco del Giglio; map p.135 C1

Prestigious gallery of modern and contemporary paintings and sculpture.

La Stamperia del Ghetto
Calle del Ghetto Vecchio

Below: Bruno Magli, for quality leather footwear.

1185/a, Cannaregio; tel: 041-275 0200; vaporetto: Guglie; map p.134 B3
Stocks prints of general Venetian themes but specialises in black-and-white prints of the Old Ghetto.

Shoes

The fact that there are so many shoe shops in Venice is due to the long tradition of shoe-making along the Brenta Canal that runs between Venice and Padua, where much of Italy's footwear is produced. Many of the best shoe-buying opportunities are to be found along the Mercerie, along with other goods such as chic bags and wallets.

Bruno Magli
Campo San Moisè, San Marco; tel: 041-522-7210; vaporetto: San Marco Vallaresso; map p.137 E2
Opposite the Hotel Bauer, Bruno Magli has well-made and mouth-watering footwear designs.

Soaps and Candles

La Calle
Campo Santa Maria del Giglio, San Marco; vaporetto: Santa Maraia del Giglio; map p.137 D2

For women, the *civetta* is a flirtatious, catlike mask while the *colombina* (which is derived from a Commedia dell'Arte character) is more ladylike.

La Calle stocks the wonderful Santa Maria Novella range of olive oil soaps, candles and scents. Prettily wrapped, they make ideal presents.

Wood

The Venetian tradition of woodwork dates back to the founding of the city when the first buildings were constructed over tightly-packed timber piles. Although not apparent in the main shopping streets, a number of specialist woodworkers survive in the city, including carpenters, cabinet makers, frame makers and furniture restorers; plus a handful of gondola craftsmen. For the ultimate Venetian souvenir splash out on a *fòrcola*, a golden oarlock made by specialist craftspeople, usually in walnut or cherry wood.

Saverio
Fondamenta Soranzo de la Fornace, Dorsoduro 341, tel: 041-522 5699; vaporetto: Salute; map p.137 D1
The best known fòrcola craftsman who makes them in all shapes and sizes.

De Marchi
Piscina San Samuele, San Marco; tel: 041-528 5694; vaporetto: San Samuele; map p.137 C3
The show-stopping window display features everyday items such as hanging jackets, hats, ties, telephones, all in carved wood. Livio de Marchi (who has something of Salvador Dalí about him) has his own motorized wooden car which can occa-

sionally be seen cruising down Venetian canals!

Markets

When it comes to markets, the best in Venice are the **Rialto** markets, which sell food of all kinds *(see Food and Drink, p.55)*. There is a good **Antiques Fair** (Mercatino dell'Antiquariato) held in the Campo San Maurizio near Campo Santo Stefano but only three times a year: on the first weekend of April, around the middle of September, and on the weekend before Christmas. Here you can find everything from genuine antiques – lace, jewellery and glassware – to old prints and photographs and quite a lot of fascinating old tat.

Below: the Rialto Market.

Transract

Venice is the only city in the world where the only form of public transport is some kind of boat. And there are several kinds to choose from: gondolas, *traghetti* (gondola ferries), *vaporetti* (water buses), water taxis and ferries to the islands in the lagoon. Once you have mastered a few key routes, water transport is quite straightforward and certainly the best way to get around far-flung parts of the city. However, most of the time you will probably be walking, which is more practical in the city centre. Exploring the narrow alleys and *campi* will familiarise you with the city and its diverse neighbourhoods as nothing else could.

Above: passenger cruise terminal.

Arriving by Air

The main airport for Venice is Marco Polo on the edge of the lagoon, 13km from the city centre. Some airlines refer to Treviso as 'Venice airport'. This is, in fact, 30km to the north of Venice and far less convenient. It's worth considering a flight-plus-hotel package to Venice, which can be cheaper. There are direct flights to Marco Polo from the major European capitals. You can fly direct from New York (JFK) or from Philadelphia but other flights from the US are usually via London, Rome, Milan, Frankfurt or Amsterdam.

From Australia and New Zealand flights are generally via Rome or Milan. Companies flying from the UK include **British Airways** (tel: 0870 850 9850; www.ba.com) and **EasyJet** (tel: 0905 821 0905; www.easyjet.com) who both operate flights from London Gatwick; **bmi** (tel: 0870 6070 555, www.flybmi.com) fly from London Heathrow; and **Ryanair** (tel: 0906 270 5656; www.ryanair.com) from London Stansted to Treviso.

For flight information at Marco Polo airport visit www.veniceairport.com; tel: 041-260 6111.

Arriving by Train

Venice is very well connected by train. The main station is Venezia–Santa Lucia (tel: 041-892021, lost property: 041-785 531). Travel time to Milan or Florence is three hours, to Rome four hours. InterRail cards are valid in Italy, as is the Eurailpass for non-European residents (buy before you leave home). The Eurodomino Pass offers travel on any three–eight day period in one month in several European countries.

Rail Europe
178 Piccadilly, London W1V 0AL; www.raileurope.co.uk.

TRENITALIA PASS

The Trenitalia Pass covering all trains in Italy is valid for unlimited travel for 4–10 days

Left: Vaporetto no. 1 on the Grand Canal.

There are any number of ways that you can 'offset' the carbon footprint of your trip to Venice, from planting a tree, to investing in sustainable technology development, to 'retiring' carbon credits, which basically means purchasing them and not using them, so they are 'retired' and no one else can buy them. If you are interested in finding out more about this, go to www.carbonfootprint.com, www.carbonplanet.com or www.begreennow.com for more information.

within a two month period. Travel on Eurostar Italia, Intercity Plus and other high-speed trains is permitted on payment of a supplement. For train information, tel: 8488-88088; www.trenitalia.it.

Arriving By Bus

Buses arrive in Venice at Piazzale Roma. There is a good, cheap bus service between Venice and nearby Padua.

On Arrival

MARCO POLO AIRPORT
From outside the terminal at Marco Polo airport, ACTV (tel: 041-272 2111, www.actv.it) run public buses to Piazzale Roma every half hour; ATVO also have a regular, slightly more expensive service (tel: 0421-383 672/1; www.atvo.it) to Piazzale Roma. The journey takes 30 minutes, ending at the terminus near the landing stage for *vaporetti* (ferries) to the centre. Alternatively, you can buy a bus or water travel pass from the VeLa office in Piazzale Roma, near the landing stage (7.30am–8pm).

Splashing out on a water taxi is a magical way to see Venice for the first time (from around €90 from the airport to the centre, but beware of extras). Or you can pre-book a water taxi from €27 per person with **Bucintoro Viaggi**; tel: +39-041-521 0632; www.bucintoroviaggi.com. There are also conventional (car) taxis (from around €30) to Piazzale Roma (tel: 041-523 7774/041-936 137).

TREVISO AIRPORT
From Treviso airport Eurobus run a service via Mestre to Piazzale Roma in Venice, taking just over an hour (€9

Below: Venice Eurostar.

return) and connecting with Ryanair flights. Tickets must be bought in the airport before boarding.

Water Transport

Ferries or water buses are known as *vaporetti*. If you arrive at Santa Lucia railway station you should buy your *vaporetto* ticket from the kiosk. Alternatively you can purchase a pass in the form of a Venicecard (with the blue version just covering transport and the orange version including access to many museums as well), though these are expensive for what they offer. There are

Vaporetti Network

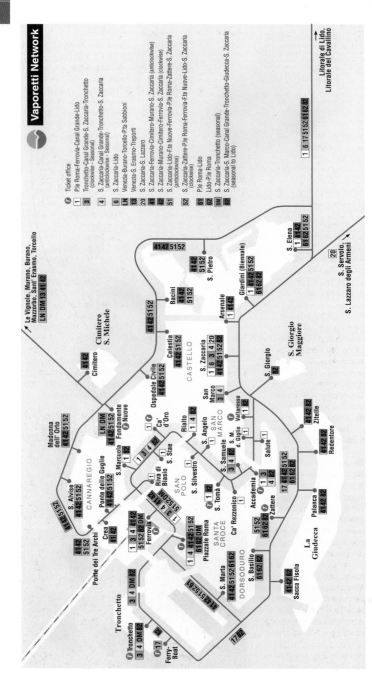

If you arrive at Piazzale Roma collect a free route-map and timetable from the ACTV offices near the landing stage.

reductions for 'juniors'; those under 29. A tiny saving can be made by purchasing online before you go to Venice (www.venice-card.com); otherwise you can buy them at Piazzale Roma and in tourist offices, among other places. Currently a one-day blue card costs €18.50 for 12 hours, €33.90 for 48 hours; or for those aged 29 and under €16.50 and €30.90; an orange card is €29.90 for 12 hours, €54.90 for 48 hours, discounted to €22.90 and €46.50 for 'juniors'.

MAIN FERRY ROUTES

Line 1 is the most romantic and the best way to get a feel of the city. It runs the length of the Grand Canal, stopping everywhere. Line 82 is the quickest way from the station to central Venice, the Lido and Giudecca, and makes fewer stops than line 1.

The most confusing landing-stages are at San Zaccaria (Riva degli Schiavoni), San Marco and Fondamente Nuove because they are spread out along the quaysides, with different services running from different jetties. The times displayed are generally reliable but double-check with a boatman if you are doubtful.

The *traghetto* is the best value public transport in Venice: a useful gondola ferry that crosses the Grand Canal at half a dozen points, saving a good deal of walking and costing just 50 cents.

Above: taking a *traghetto* to the Rialto.

FERRIES TO THE ISLANDS

For the main islands: to San Giorgio Maggiore, take line 82; for Giudecca, 41, 42, 82; for the Lido, lines 1, 51, 52, 61, 62, 82; for Murano, 41, 42 and LN (Laguna Nord), for Burano and Torcello LN.

For the smaller islands, always double-check return times before setting out, as these ferries can be fairly infrequent and you don't want to be stranded. For San Servolo and Lazzaro degli Armeni take line 20; for San Francesco del Deserto, take LN (Laguna Nord) to Burano, then get a water taxi; for San Michele, known as Cimitero, lines 41 or 42; for Sant'Erasmo, line 13 from Fondamente Nuove.

For current information on ferries, tel: 041-2424.

Water Taxis

If you want to travel in style, pick up an expensive water-taxi on the taxi stand on Riva degli Schiavoni, near San Marco (tel: 041-522 2303/041-522 9750).

Gondolas

Gondola rides are expensive, but taking one of them is an essential part of the Venice experience and most people think they are worth the money. The city sets official rates, (currently €80 for 40 minutes, up to 6 people, climbing to €100 after 7pm with extra charges for music). However, some gondoliers will disregard the official rates or shorten your ride. Always agree a price and a route with the gondolier in advance (or get your hotel concierge to do it for you if you're willing to pay a commission), but, for romance, stick to the peaceful side canals rather than the Grand Canal. You can find gondolas at the main tourist areas, from Tronchetto and the Piazzale Roma to the Rialto Bridge area, the Doge's Palace, and at busy pedestrian crossings along the side-canals. Serenaded gondola tours may sound cheesy, but they can be magical. Information on these is available from most travel agents.

131

Walks

A lthough Venice is a city built on water, it doesn't mean you have to walk on water to get around; except at times of *aqua alta* (high water) in winter, when that is exactly what you do need to do in the Piazza San Marco. Venice is, in fact, a delightful city to explore on foot, partly because it has the huge advantage of being traffic-free. Away from the tourist hotspots, you can meander along quiet canals, stroll down alleys that lead into quaint neighbourhood *campi*, and generally just enjoy losing yourself in the labyrinth. A few good walks are outlined here, but you are sure to discover more if you just follow your nose.

Dorsoduro: the Zattere

Dorsoduro is the most attractive quarter for idle wandering, with wisteria-clad walls, secret gardens and distinctive domestic architecture. The southern spur of the Zattere makes the most enchanting promenade, bracing in winter and refreshing in summer. The Punta della Dogana, the Sea Customs Point on the triangular tip of Dorsoduro, is the start of this popular walk. From here, the Zattere stretches all the way round the southern shore, its quaysides flanked by churches, boathouses, warehouses and a string of inviting open-air cafés. At the first sign of spring sunshine, Venetian sun-worshippers flock to the landing stages and decks that line the shore. Summer *passeggiate* are also de rigueur, partly to cómbat the heat and city claustrophobia, partly to parade the latest fashions and sip drinks in chic cafés.

Tiepolo Trail

Dorsoduro is dotted with Tiepolo sites, shrines to the greatest Rococo artist. This

Above: losing yourself in the backstreets and alleys is a great way to experience the real Venice.

master of scenic illusion produced a riot of picturesque detail to seduce the most casual observer.

Start at **Ca' Rezzonico**, to admire his frescoed ceilings, then make your way, via Campo San Barnaba and Rio Terrà Canal to Campo di Santa Margherita, where you can enjoy Tiepolo's sensuous *Madonna of the Scapular* in the **Scuola Grande dei Carmini**. Head south to the Zattere via Calle de le Pazienze, Rio Terà Ognissanti and Calle Trevisan. Turn left

for the **Gesuati** church, with illusionistic frescoes and a joyous altarpiece by Tiepolo. SEE ALSO CHURCHES, P.44; PALAZZI, P.99–100; SCUOLE, P.121

Cannaregio: the Ghetto and Madonna dell'Orto

Start at the Campo del Ghetto Nuovo (New Ghetto Square) which, despite its name, stands at the heart of the world's oldest ghetto, a fortified island created in 1516. This moated *campo* contains evocative testaments to the deportation of

Left: foreign students enjoying the view towards San Marco.

Guided tours of synagogues depart hourly from the Museo della Comunità Ebraico, from 10.30am–4.30pm (5.30pm in summer).

witness to the Rialto's mercantile past, with names such as *olio* (oil), *vino* (wine), *spezie* (spices), *polli* (poultry) and *beccarie* (meat). Ruga degli Orefici, Goldsmiths' Street, begins at the foot of the Rialto Bridge, while Ruga degli Speziali, Spice Traders' Street is nearby. Today, smelly alleys often triumph over spicy perfumes, but the market is rarely squalid and makes a refreshing change from the monumental Venice of San Marco. The real heart of the market remains the fruit and vegetable vendors around the Campo San Giacomo di Rialto and the 'Pescaria'. The Rialto remains a hive of commercial activity, with everything you could wish for on sale between here and the Mercerie in the San Marco district, and there are lots of tempting little *bacari*, the traditional wine bars.

The down-to-earth Rialto market is one of the few places in the city where the Italian language prevails, along with the guttural sing-song of Venetian dialect.

Jews, in the form of memorial plaques under symbolic strips of barbed wire. Three of Venice's five remaining synagogues are set around the square, as unobtrusive as the Ghetto itself. Although hidden behind nondescript façades, the synagogues reveal lavish interiors. One of them is above the **Museo della Comunità Ebraico** (Jewish Museum). Head north from the square, crossing the bridge for Fondamenta degli Ormesini. A left and right turn will bring you to Fondamenta della Sensa, with the Campo dei Mori, named after the oriental figures carved on the campo walls. Tintoretto's house (no. 3399) lies just along the waterfront. Several of his paintings can be seen in the lovely Gothic church of **Madonna dell'Orto** just to the north, where the artist is

buried. Take time to explore this picturesque neighbourhood of northern Venice before taking a *vaporetto* back to central Venice from the Madonna dell'Orto landing stage.

SEE ALSO CHURCHES, P.42; MUSEUMS AND GALLERIES, P.81

The Rialto

Treading the labyrinthine alleys of the Rialto is an intoxicating experience, especially in the morning. The alleys and quays bear

Below: sunset lagoon crossing.

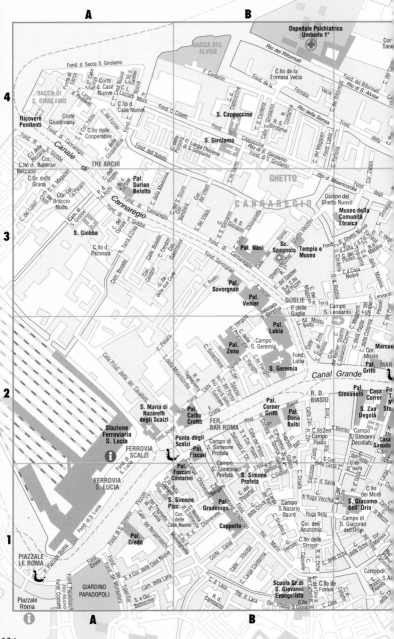

S. ALVISE

SECCHIERE

S. Alvise

MADONNA DELL'ORTO

C a n a l e   d e l l e   N a v i

Sacca della Misericordia

Madonna dell' Orto

Casino d. Spiriti

Pal. Michiel

Pal. Minelli

Pal. Contarini d. Zaffo

Campo della Madonna dell'Orto

Pal. Mastelli

Casa del Tintoretto

Pal. Longo

P. della Sacca

Ex Conv. S.M. d. Servi

S. Marziale

S. M. Valverde

Pal. Diedo

Cam. del' Abbazia

Pal. Lezze

P. S. Antonio

Campo di S. Fosca

Pal. Vendramin

Pal. Fosca

S. Maddalena

Pal. Correr

Pal. Molin

S. Caterina

Pal. Papafava

Pal. Zen

S. Maria Assunta dei Gesuiti

Campo dei Gesuiti

Orat. d. Crociferi

Pal. endramin-Calergi

Pal. Soranzo

Pal. Erizzo

Pal. Giovanelli

Pal. Molin

Pal. Emo

Dep. d. Megio

Pal. Priuli S.

Pal. Tron

Pal. Barbarigo Zulian

P. Pasqualigo

S. Felice

Pal. Gussoni

S. Stae

Pal. Foscarini

Ca' Pesaro

Gall. d'Arte Mod. & Mus. Orient.

Pal. Boldù

Pal. Fontana

Gall. Franchetti

Ca' d'Oro

S. Sofia

S. Maria Mater Dom.

Pal. Mocenigo

Pal. Agnus Dio

Casa Favretto

Pal. Brandolin

CA' D'ORO

Pal. Foscari

Pal. Sagredo

Pal. Michiel d. Colonne

Scuola di S. Ang. Custode

SS. Apostoli

Cor. del Remer

Cor. Contarini

Campo di S. Maddalena

Campo S. Maria Mater Domini

Pal. Gozzi

S. Cassiano

Pal. Muti Baglioni

Pal. Querini

Pescheria

Campo della Pescaria

Fabbriche Nuove

Valmarana

Ca' da Mosto

S. Canciano

S. Canciano

Campo S. Canciano

Boldù

S. Maria dei Miracoli

Pal. Sanudo

Fabbriche Vecchie

S. Giov. Cristosomo

Teatro Malibran

Pal. Amadi

Pal. Bragadin Carabba

Pal. delle Tette

Casa di B. Cappello

S. Giovanni Elemosinario

C.S. Giacomo di Rialto

Pal. dei Camer-lenghi

Pal. Civran

Pal. Bernardo

p134 p135 p139 p136 p137 p140

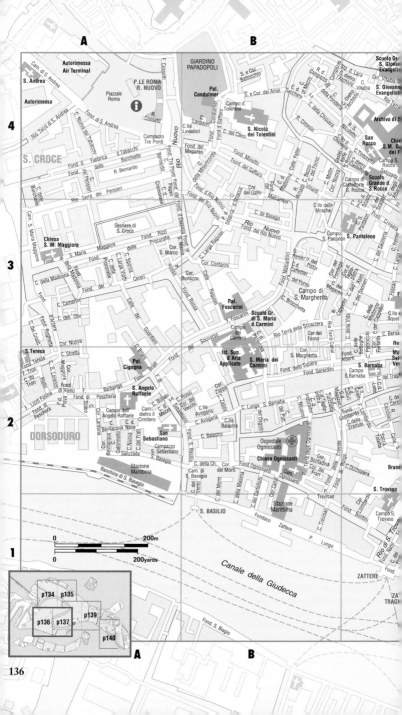

A   B

4

Cam. di S. Andrea
Air Terminal
Autorimessa
S. Andrea
Autorimessa
Cam. di S. Andrea
Fond. di S. Andrea
Rio Terra di S. Andrea
C. Nuova dei Tabacchi
Fond. d. Fabbrica
delle Burchielle
R. Bernardo
Fond. d. Pensieri
Cam. di S. Maria Maggiore
Fond. delle Burchielle

S. CROCE

P.LE ROMA
R. NUOVO
Piazzale
Roma
ℹ
Campazzo
Tre Ponti
Fond. Tre Ponti
Bernardo
Rio Terra dei Pensieri

F. Cossetti
R. Cossetti
Rio Nuovo
C. Lavadori
C.llo Lavadori
Fond. del Magazen
Fond. della Misericordia

GIARDINO
PAPADOPOLI
Pal.
Condulmer
Campo d.
Tolentini
S. Nicolò
dei Tolentini
Fond. Condulmer
R. del Gaffaro
C. del Clero
Fond. Minotto
Fond. del Gaffaro
Fond. d. Rio Nuovo
Cor. del Gallo
Malcanton

R. d. Sto. d. Laca
C. dietro
Archivio
R. del Magazzo
C. della Fonderia
R. di Vitalba
R. Chiovere
Sto. e Cor. dei Amai
Sto. e Cor. dei Amai
R. Clinesin
Madonna, Calle Taller
Calle d. Forno
Amai
C. Vinanti
Cor. del Forno
Bari d. Forno

Scuola Gr.
S. Giovan
Evangelis
Cor. Vitalba, S.
S. Giovanni
Evangelist
Rio Terra
Archivio di S
San
Rocco
Chie
S.M. G.
dei F
Campo S.
Rocco
Scuola
Grande d.
S. Rocco
C.llo delle
Mosche

3

Chiesa
S. M. Maggiore
Fond. di S. Maria Maggiore
C. della Madonna
Fond. della Madonna
C. Camerini
C. dell' Olio
Sesriere di
S. Croce
Fond. Rizzi
Fond. delle Procuratie
Cal. Larga Viona
C. Sforza
delle Procuratie
Cor. Bottazzo
Cor. Contarini
Cor. Larga Ragusa
Cal. Rafaela
Calle del
Rosso

RIO
NUOVO
Fond. del Rio Nuovo
Campo
S. Pantalon
S. Pantaleon
Renier o. del Pistor
C. d. Caffettier
Cor. del Forno
Campo di
S. Margherita
C. Brocchetta
Cor. del Tentor
Cal. Pedrocchi
Cappella

2

S. Teresa
C. Teresa
F. Tron
C.llo Tron
Fond. d'Arzere
C. del Cristo
Fond. Rughetta
Cor. Nuova
C. Camerini
C. Stretta
S. Lorenzo
C. Maggiore
Fond. di Riello
C. di
Priore
Fond. di
Pescaria
Barbarigo
Campo dell'
Angelo Raffaele
Cor. Lardona
Calomelato
Cor. Nuova
C. del Fabri
Corte
Salizzada
Bevilacqua Nave

Pal.
Cigogna
S. Angelo
Raffaele
Cam. dietro il
Cimitero
San
Sebastiano
Campazzo
S. Sebastiano
C. della Ch.
Cam. di
S. Basegio

Pal.
Foscarini
Scuola Gr.
di S. Maria
d. Carmini
Campo
dei
Carmini
C. Foscarini
Rio Terra della Scoazzera
Ist. Sup.
d'Arte
Applicate
S. Maria dei
Carmini
Fond. dello Squero
Cor.
Zappa
C. Rossi
Cor. delle
Vecchie
C.llo
Avogaria
C. Avogaria
C. Balastro
Ospedale
Ognissanti
✚
Chiesa Ognissanti
Fond. Ognissanti
Cam.
Ognissanti

Cor. del
Forno
Fond. Gerardini
Cor.
Margherita
Fond. S. Barnaba
Campo
S. Barnaba
C. Lunga S. Barnaba
Cor.
Zappa
C. Nardo
Fond. Eremite
Cor. del
Brenta
Fond. Bonfadina
Fond. dei
Frari
Fond. Ognissanti
Rio Terra degli Ognissanti

C. del Saloni
S. Pantaleon
C. della Vida
Fond. delle
Botteghe
S. Barnaba
Campo
S. Barnaba
Mu
Sel
Ven
C. Berna
Re
C.llo
Squel
Brand
S. Trovaso
Campo S.
Trovaso
Rio di S. Trov

1

0   200m
0   200yards

Stazione
Marittima
Banchina di S. Basegio
C. del Vento
Cor. dei Morti
Fond. Ognissanti
Stazione
Marittima

C. della Masena
Trevisan
Fondaco
Zattere
P. Lungo

S. BASILIO

Canale della Giudecca

Fond. S. Biagio

ZATTERE
ZA
TRAGI

DORSODURO

p134 | p135
p136 | p137 | p139
p140

A   B

136

D

E

0   200m

0   200yards

p134   p135

p138   p139

p136

p140

4

S. Lazzaro
Mendicanti

 spedale
Civile

OSPEDALE CIVILE

S. Maria
del Pianto

CELESTIA

S. Giovanni
Paolo

Ospedale
dei Vecchi

S. Maria
dei Derelitti

Fond. Case Nuove

P. Assisi

C. 2ª

C. Sagredo

Fond. Case Nuove

Barbaria delle Tole

Cor. delle
Muneghe

C. d. Maddonetta

C. dei Caffetier

R.
della Mosca

Moschette

Calle Cavalli

Calle Capuccine

Fond. Giustina

Campo
S. Francesco
della Vigna

S. Francesco
della Vigna

Cimitero

C. Sagredo

C. del Oratorio

C. 2ª

C. Crimitera

Cor. delle
Galeazze

3

C. Mazzor

C. S. Francesco

Convento

Campo della
Confraternità

Campo
della
Celestia

Arsenale

S. Giustina
di Barbaria

S. Giustina

Campo
Te Deum

Pal.
Gradenigo

C. Francesco

Canale delle Galeazze

S. Lorenzo

Salizzada S. Giustina

Cor.
Cappallera

Cor.
Morlon

Cor.
Vida

Campo
S. Ternita

Borgoloco S. Lorenzo

C. Larga S. Lorenzo

Campo
S. Lorenzo

Cor.
Nuova

C.d. Vida

P. Scoazzera

Questura

C. S. Lorenzo

C. Sacca

Salizzada S. Lorenzo

C. dell'Olio

C. Magno

Arsenale

Scuola di
S. Giorgio degli
Schiavoni

Campo
delle Gatte

C. del Lion

C. dei Furlani

C. Drazzi

Darsena Arsenale Vecchio

Pal.
Priuli

C. dei Preti

Pal. Zorzi

C. Maruzzi

C. della Madonna

Calle dei Furlani

C.llo Due
Pozzi

C. Mandoli

Campo
delle
Gorne

Arsenale

Fond. dell'

Osmarin

C. del Magazen

Mus. dell'Inst.
Ellénico

Sal. dei Greci

S. Antonio

C. dell'Arco

C. delle
Porte

C. Maria

Cor.
Soranzo

Campo
della Grana

Darsena
Grande

S. Giorgio
dei Greci

Campo
S. Antonin

Cor.
Bosello

Cor.
Bollani

Salizzada S. Antonin

P. dei
Penini

Cor.
Soranzo

2

Campo
S. Zaccaria

San
Zaccaria

Rio dei Greci

C.
dietro la Pietà

Cor.
Terrazzera

Campo
Bandiera
e Moro già
della Bragora

C. d'Drazzi

S. Antonin

C.llo
Pestrin

C. del Pestrin

Portal des
Arsenale

C. Forni

Fond. dell'Arsenale

S. Martino

Campo
dell'
Arsenale

Fond. della Madonna

CASTELLO

Arsenale

S. Maria
della Pietà

Pal.
Navagero

C. della Pietà

S. Giovanni
in Bragora

C.llo
del Piovan

C. Erizzo

C. s. Gioan

C. Pescaria

Morosina

Fond. Rio Nuovo

C. d.
Pegola

C. d.
Malvasia

C. d.
Pegola

Schiavoni

Riva

degli

Schiavoni

PIETÀ

S. ZACCARIA
DANIELI

RIVA
DEGLI SCHIAVONI

Instituto
Ca' di Dio

C. delle
Vele

Fond. dell'Arsenale

Campo
della Tana

della   Tana

Rio
Cor. Grimani

S. ARIA
DA

CARIA

Riva di Ca' di Dio

ARSENALE

Museo
Navale

Campo
S. Biagio

S. Biagio

Riva S. Biagio

Via G. Garibaldi

C. del Santi

S. Pietro
o Piedricastic

1

Canale   di   San   Marco

Schiavoni

D

E

139

Selective Index for Street Atlas

Index

Insight Smart Guide: Venice

Text by: Lisa Gerard-Sharp

Compiled by: Pam Barrett

Edited by: Maria Lord

Proofread and indexed by: Erica Brown

Photography by: 4-Corners 50C, 87B
akg-images, London 5TR, 36, 52C, 56B, 59T&CT, 75B,
77T, 78, 80, 81T&B, 82B, 83, 84C, 100; Alamy 86B,
89T, 126/127T, 129B; Art Archive 58B; Bridgeman Art
Library 68/69T, 74/75T, 82T, 90/91T; Ca'Pisani 63; Cor-
bis 27T, 46/47T, 52/53T, 53B, 57B, 59CB, 68C, 84/85T,
88, 104/105T; Danieli 62, 110; Glyn Genin/Apa 4TL,
5C&CR, 6, 7T, 8, 11T, 15B, 21T, 26, 27B, 28/29T, 37T,
43, 44B, 49B, 51B, 59B, 70C, 70/71T, 71B, 73, 74C,
101T, 105B&L, 116/117T, 118C, 119B, 120T&B, 121,
124, 125BR, 133B; Getty Images 46C, 50/51T, 56/57T;
Grand Hotel des Bains 60/61T, 115; Gritti Palace 60B,
107B; Benjamin W.G. Legde 58T&CT; Mary Evans Picture
Library 58CB, 69B; Ros Miller/Apa 11B, 20, 28C, 39B,
41T, 44T, 66T, 79B, 117B; Anna Mockford & Nick
Bonetti/Apa 2B, 2/3T, 4B, 5TL&BL, 7B, 9B, 10,12,
13T&B, 14, 15T, 16, 17T, 18, 19T&B, 21B, 22, 23T&B,
25T&B, 29B, 30B, 30/31T, 31B, 32, 33, 34T&B,
35TL,TR&B, 37B, 38/39T, 41T&B, 42T, 45B, 47B, 48C,
48/49T, 54BL,BC& BR, 54/55T, 55B, 66CT,CB&B,

66/67T, 67B, 72BL&BR, 76, 77B, 85B, 86/87T, 89B,
92B, 92/93T, 93B, 95, 96, 97BL&BR, 99T&B, 101B,
102B, 104C, 105BR, 106C, 106/107T, 108T,
108/109B, 109T, 111T&B, 112, 113, 114, 116C, 122C,
122/123T, 125BL, 126B, 127B, 128C, 128/129T, 131,
132C, 132/133T; Orient Express Images 64, 65;
102/103T, 103B; R. Solomon Guggenheim Foundation
79T; V&A Images 123B; Bill Wassman 98

Picture Manager: Hilary Genin

Maps: James Macdonald

Series Editor: Maria Lord

First Edition 2008

© 2008 Apa Publications GmbH & Co. Verlag KG Singapore Branch, Singapore.

Printed in Singapore by Insight Print Services
(Pte) Ltd

Worldwide distribution enquiries:

**Apa Publications GmbH & Co. Verlag KG
(Singapore Branch)** 38 Joo Koon Road, Singapore 628990; tel: (65) 6865 1600; fax:
(65) 6861 6438

Distributed in the UK and Ireland by:

GeoCenter International Ltd
Meridian House, Churchill Way West, Bas-
ingstoke, Hampshire RG21 6YR; tel: (44

1256) 817 987; fax: (44 1256) 817 988

Distributed in the United States by:

Langenscheidt Publishers, Inc.
36–36 33rd Street Fourth Floor, Long Island
City, New York 11106; tel: (1 718) 784
0055; fax: (1 718) 784 0640I

Contacting the Editors

We would appreciate it if readers would alert
us to outdated information by writing to:
**Apa Publications, PO Box 7910, London
SE1 1WE, UK; fax: (44 20) 7403 0290;
e-mail: insight@apaguide.co.uk**

No part of this book may be reproduced,
stored in a retrieval system or transmitted in
any form or by any means (electronic,
mechanical, photocopying, recording or otherwise), without prior written permission of
Apa Publications. Brief text quotations with
use of photographs are exempted for book
review purposes only. Information has been
obtained from sources believed to be reliable, but its accuracy and completeness,
and the opinions based thereon, are not
guaranteed.